D0530217

acting**characters**

20 essential steps from rehearsal to performance

2nd edition

acknowledgements

The author would like to thank the following for their help with this book: Anna Brewer, Sarah Hughes, Sybil Eysenck, Jenny Ridout, Alan Ayckbourn, Heather Stoney, Gemma Albon, Ben Kingsley.

For Amy, Mike and Chris

acting**characters**

20 essential steps from rehearsal to performance

2nd edition

paul elsam

methuen | drama

Methuen Drama

1 3 5 7 9 10 8 6 4 2

Methuen Drama is an imprint of Bloomsbury Publishing Plc

Methuen Drama
Bloomsbury Publishing Plc
36 Soho Square
London W1D 3QY
www.methuendrama.com

First edition published in 2006
Second edition published in 2011

A CIP catalogue record for this book is available from the
British Library

ISBN: 978 1 408 13284 5

Typeset by Margaret Brain
Printed and bound in Great Britain by CPI Cox & Wyman

contents

foreword to the second edition

Having never formally trained as an actor, I remain forever indebted to the writers, actors and directors with whom I took my first steps. I first worked in Theatre in Education, guided by the visionary Brian Way. It was my first job as an actor and I clearly recall the encouragement given to me by a radiantly pregnant young director who told me outright that I would 'be a great classical actor'. I was overwhelmed both by her and her conviction. She addressed her remarks to the young actor struggling in the rehearsal room guided only by his intuition. Her words were both a profound embrace and a warning, the subtext of her praises being 'you are going to have to work very, very hard'.

My journey beyond her was blessed, as Brian Way knew Stephen Joseph of Scarborough and he in turn knew Peter Cheeseman of Stoke-on-Trent's famous Victoria Theatre-in-the-round, and it was indeed Peter who offered me my second job. It was through Peter and Stephen that I met and worked with the great Sir Alan Ayckbourn. Both my first two jobs involved us actors performing in the round: no hiding place.

I write all this because I am compelled to quote my friend Alan Ayckbourn in saying, 'There's a lot of nonsense written about acting', and the wonderful Tilda Swinton said much the same thing only not quotable in these pages due to the expletives her anger prompted her to use. I get angry, too, at the utter nonsense written and talked about acting. I get saddened when I see young actors imprisoned in a bogus set of 'acting coach' rules whilst strangling their own intuition.

Acting is a reflection and demonstration of our collective knowledge of the human soul. It is an extension of the healing art of story telling. It is more pure and more simple than many would have us believe. A mature director will work with what is literally in front of his or her eyes in the rehearsal room or on set; work with the actors as they truly are, not as the director would wish them to be.

So the crucial gift or talent the beginning actor must be blessed with is a profound sense of the joy of story telling, whether that story be the incandescent tragedy of *Hamlet* or the glorious vulnerability of *Bedroom Farce*.

The techniques offered by Paul Elsam in this book are all aimed at lending strength and skill to the young actor's intuition. Often the gulf between what we wish to express in performance and what we are barely capable of in rehearsal can seem unbridgeable. This book offers graspable steps towards bridging that seemingly unbridgeable gap through exercises that will strengthen concentration, physical stamina, vocal flexibility and confidence.

It is, above all, a generous book. It does not seek to clutter the actor with 'nonsense' but to equip the actor with the technical tools necessary to be seen and heard in our crowded arena.

Sir Ben Kingsley

foreword to the first edition

There's a lot of nonsense written about acting, much of it by people who have never acted or spent any time with someone who does. It's good to welcome a practical uncluttered book written by someone who has done both.

Similarly, writing as one who spent the first eight years of his working life pursuing a faltering acting career and the next forty as a director trying to help others to do the job better, I feel I know a little about the subject.

I have, after all, spent years of my life in rehearsal rooms, day after day watching the acting process (and more importantly what leads up to the acting process), first hand. Sometimes this can be laborious (like watching paint dry); at other times, it's instinctively swift and near miraculous, witnessing one personality melt into another.

Yet if that all sounds rather mystical, whatever route the actor takes towards a finished interpretation, in the right company, with the right fellow actors, text, director and the reassuring safety net of good technical support from the other departments, it's also enormous fun.

True, acting entails a great deal of patience, application and sheer hard work, make no mistake, and I know it is rather frowned upon to link hard work with fun, certainly in this country. But the two, surely, need not – should not – be mutually exclusive.

Acting is one of those extraordinary, sometimes frustrating jobs wherein the less of it you seem to be doing, the better you appear to be doing it.

As, I suspect, is true with most art. Many of the greatest achievements are produced joyously, as if guided by instinct. Likewise some of the dullest work is the result of painful grind and endless hard labour – and it shows. We may faintly applaud the obvious huge effort put into it all but nonetheless we soon turn away or leave at the interval.

So, aspiring actor-to-be who may be planning to read this book, always trust your instincts first and foremost. However good you are, they will be proven wrong once in a while but as long as you don't get immovably entrenched, you can always retract later. And if your first instincts do prove unfailingly wrong more often than not, then perhaps you should start pursuing a different career, as I did.

Paul Elsam is a former actor who now teaches and directs. His approach is technical and refreshingly non-academic. He charts clear and helpful pathways to guide the student actor towards a performance, which can be very useful, believe me. In choosing to become a professional actor you are, in return for an often pitiful renumeration, contracted to produce something watchable and stageworthy within a finite time to perform over a finite period. Sometimes, long before rehearsals have finished or even started, people have already paid good money for their seats.

And no matter how good your instincts, in the end you will also need a surefire practical technique to fall back on. In this book, Paul quite rightly makes the point that good actors are well aware it is not possible to be at the height of their game every night, eight times a week, month in month out. There will be days when 'inspiration' deserts them. Those are the days when technique comes into play to compensate for this. And, if you get to be really good, most people will never tell the difference.

Sir Alan Ayckbourn

introduction

What is your technique for creating a character? What indeed is a character?

The very concept of the actor's character in drama is quite a controversial one. Since Konstantin Stanislavski wrote *Building a Character* in the early twentieth century, generations of actors have pursued the mercurial task of capturing the essence of their character. Yet playwright and director David Mamet among others asserts passionately that there is no such thing as a character, just an actor, whose simple task is to serve the play in the manner prescribed by the playwright.

There are of course traps for the actor who wants to be able to create a character. There is the seductive urge to make the character memorable and interesting, which can lead to all sorts of questionable character choices ranging from a slight stammer to a tendency to scratch without reason. There is the temptation to lead your character off in an emotional direction which feels artistically satisfying, but happens to run counter to the play. There is the simple danger that the more you delve into your own character, the less you may notice those around you.

Alan Ayckbourn tells the story of when he was a young actor rehearsing the role of Stanley in *The Birthday Party*, under the direction of playwright Harold Pinter. Keen to do a good job, Alan badgered Harold for nuggets of information about his mysterious character. Harold calmly told him to 'mind your own ****ing business'.

The bottom line is that the most interesting, spontaneous, responsive and three-dimensional character you can harness is you. This is quite handy because if you basically play yourself, as some actors do, you can put all of your energy into responding truthfully to situations encountered in the play. It's common today, especially in television and film, for a casting director to put someone forward for a part precisely because the actor so closely resembles the appearance and personality of the character in the script. If you think you've been cast for this reason, you'd be well advised to keep your character work simple and just deliver the goods. Once your employers know that you're reliable and can act truthfully, they may take a bit more of a risk with you next time.

So are there still opportunities for the actor who enjoys playing different people – who wants to be what we might call a 'transformational character actor'? Thankfully, yes. Theatre can still offer real character acting challenges, especially if you're cast to play more than one role in the same piece – something which is now fairly common due to shrinking theatre budgets. In a typical early John Godber play you may be called on to play numerous roles including some stereotypes, all of which need to be markedly different. And there are other areas of employment for transformational character actors – the corporate video sector, radio plays, the live role-play sector within business – all of which require the actor to be something of a chameleon.

You will want in rehearsal to add something of your own to a role. The director will want to ensure that your choices make sense within the parameters of the play. To balance these two 'wants', you will need, above all, a clear eye and a strong, versatile technique. But where to find that technique?

Stanislavski's teaching

Some of the tips I offer in this book spring from the advice of **Konstantin Stanislavski**. Early in the last century Stanislavski mapped out a comprehensive system for actor training, and his work still forms the cornerstone for pretty much all modern actor training in the West. He teaches how to make a script more easily digestible by dividing it into units. He also teaches about circles of attention, tempo-rhythm in the voice and tempo-rhythm in the body, emotion memory, and all sorts of tricks, techniques and exercises. His system has, like that other best-seller the Bible, been quoted and misquoted and re-written and 'improved'; but it has for sure helped many actors find their way. Some, including David Mamet, think Stanislavski has created a baffling system which has harmed actors' ability to act well. Others (myself included) feel that although Stanislavski wrote much which is still of value to actors, some of his writings now seem remote. There was a thrilling period in the early days of naturalistic theatre, in the late nineteenth century, when actors and playwrights were at times ahead of those new scientists – the psychologists – in understanding human behaviour. But some of Stanislavski's general observations on human behaviour, and how to replicate it, are perhaps less relevant now in the twenty-first century than they were when written. And while much has been added by talented and well-meaning disciples, some of them really have further muddied the water.

Horses for courses, as the saying goes. If you're attracted to the task of understanding Stanislavski's vision of acting – or those of his disciples (or rivals) – and you're willing to work systematically through the various layers of those onions, then your rewards may be rich indeed. Be aware, though, that these are demanding disciplines, and as such they tend to require an intense intellectual commitment from the pupil. It can be healthy for actors, and for their teachers, to engage with philosophies and psychologies which seem heavyweight and important – the intensive study which they demand can at best lead to excellent discipline and a confidence-boosting sense of elevated status. At worst though, they can lead to a secret sense of inadequacy, buried under an overblown sense of elevated status.

I doubt then that actors need to be academics. Clear thinkers, yes; researchers, of course; collectors, definitely. Over the years I've talked with a number of creative people working at the very top of their discipline. In every case I've been struck by their humour, their love of their craft, and their commitment to the demystification of their craft. I love that. It's inclusive; it allows people to talk about things without feeling that they have to join a secret society or develop extra brain power.

So is this book for you? Well, not if you're looking for another secret society to join. But if you already have the actor's basic talent for looking and sounding spontaneous at the drop of a hat and you'd like to become much more versatile – if you'd like to learn how to change with the ease of a chameleon – then read on. What this book is intended to deliver is a common-sense, jargon-free, step-by-step guide to help you act characters truthfully.

Transformational character acting

The book is, therefore, mostly about communication – the things people do that others can see and hear. These things tell us what someone is thinking and feeling; they help us to understand the relationship between two people; they help us to recognise how someone feels about their surroundings. The signs a person gives out through their body and their voice give us all the clues we need to understand them. So what are these signs?

We will consider all the key characteristics of behaviour — real, changeable, everyday human behaviour, both vocal and physical. You'll be guided through an understanding of the things you do in everyday life; you'll learn how, and why, you change your behaviour as a result of changing circumstances. With each behaviour 'type' you'll be offered a precise description of the behaviour including behavioural opposites and examples from the animal world. You will learn subtler versions of the behaviour and you'll see glimpses of how changes of behaviour are often used by writers and actors for comic or dramatic effect. Finally, you'll be given practical advice on how to use your new aware-ness of each behaviour when developing a character, and you will be guided through simple, practical exercises to help you sharpen your skill and awareness, and thus your versatility.

Will this book then turn you into a skilful transformational character actor? I hope so. At the very least I believe that through reading the book, and through exploring its ideas via the exercises, you'll become a more confident and sophisticated communicator. All actors engage in the task of actively creating stories for an audience. Whether actors choose to do so by using their own personality, or whether they prefer to melt away their own personality and create a new one to fit the story, is largely up to actor and director. It's certainly valid for actors to seek out and develop, in the part given, all the things which audiences need to know. And sometimes actors will be asked to inhabit a world foreign to them. What's important is that actors' choices towards the role they develop are honourable and that they do justice to the character.

To do justice to a character, though, you will need to do justice to the play. You will need to use good detective skills to work out what is going on, and to identify how your character dovetails with the rest of the characters in the play. You will need to plan. And part of your planning is to establish precisely what type of acting you need to present to your audience. In my experience actors lean towards one of three 'types'; I call these the **Inhabiter**, the **Storyteller**, and the **Classicist**.

Inhabiter actors need to 'become' a character. This type of actor works really hard to engage psychologically and emotionally with the moment-to-moment circumstances within a character's story. If you're acting onstage or on set with an Inhabiter, it feels very personal – they can draw you in, heightening the authenticity of your own performance. At best, Inhabiters are deeply moving for an audience to observe. At worst, they can resent an audience's presence, which can hamper their willingness to reach the audience with good technique. Inhabiters performing solo (e.g. delivering an audition speech) are most comfortable with a monologue that includes a second, provocative (though of course invisible) onstage character existing in the same world as the actor's character. The Inhabiter uses the power of their imagination to try as far as possible to materialise the other character onstage. This means, of course, that the other (invisible) character has an autonomy and life of their own – they may move around the stage, sit, be still, start to speak (only to be interrupted by the Inhabiter's continuing monologue). The other character has, in other words, their own wants and limitations (also known as 'objectives and barriers' – we'll be exploring these later). The depth of engagement with an imaginary world that an Inhabiter can achieve can make them highly watchable – charismatic, even. But the Inhabiter needs to remember the audience, empathise with them, and help them out with excellent vocal and physical communication.

Storyteller actors love to tell the story of the play to the audience. Even if they never actually look at the audience, they're always very aware of them, reaching through the divide to share their character's experience. Watch a Storyteller as an audience member and you'll often feel they might just catch your eye. Act with a Storyteller and you'll always feel reminded of the presence of an audience. From the audience's perspective, at best, Storytellers can be exhilarating and hugely entertaining performers. At worst, they can lack engagement with fellow actors and can lack a level of truthfulness in performance. Physical theatre – the minimalist genre of performance that requires actors to shape-shift in front of the audience typically by 'becoming' objects – demands a direct line of communication between actor and audience that suits Storyteller actors better than Inhabiter actors. Storytellers performing solo (e.g. delivering an audition speech) are most comfortable with a monologue in which the audience can, as an ensemble, be given the role of the second, responding character. The Storyteller uses the power of their imagination to help the audience to collectively accept this imposed role. This means, of course, that this 'other' character – personified by the whole audience or at least by individuals within the audience – is granted a degree of autonomy. While they cannot physically move, they are expected to listen, to mentally react, to even consider speaking (only to be interrupted by the Storyteller's continuing monologue). The audience's character is, then, granted a degree of free will, if not their own explicit wants and limitations. A Storyteller actor who can persuade an audience to commit psychologically and emotionally to an imaginary world can become very powerful. But the Storyteller working within a scene, rather than performing a monologue, needs to work hard to remember their fellow actors.

Classicist actors are drawn to what might be called poetic text – image-rich text written in a non-naturalistic style (e.g. in rhyming verse) that can be challenging to deliver. The Classicist is comfortable with the textual style of poetic performance work – including William Shakespeare, Arthur Miller in more classical mode (e.g. in parts of *The Crucible*) or indeed the poetic street verse of playwrights such as Steven Berkoff. A Classicist performer combines three elements: direct audience engagement, the delivery of difficult text and the sincere performance of a fictional character. As such, the Classicist actor performing in a play combines the skills of both the Inhabiter and the Storyteller, unravelling a character's story truthfully while skilfully 'hand-holding' their audience. At worst, they can over-indulge in the poetic nature of the text, 'charming' us with their speaking while obscuring the story with a showboating style. Their skill combines the best of the other two styles, but adds a sense of fearlessness towards 'difficult' text.

In this Section we will be considering the range and type of skills an actor needs to operate effectively. This Skills Inventory offers you the chance to see how you measure up for the job of acting, and makes suggestions on where to seek further help if you need it.

What then are the qualities you would need, in order to function as an effective professional? Before the first line is spoken in the rehearsal room, before you've even thought about character, before, indeed, the first CV and photo are to be posted, what should a professional actor be capable of doing?

For me, there are **nine such essential skills** necessary for any successful actor:

1 **knowing how to achieve a state of full physical and mental relaxation**

2 **being able to work creatively with stamina, determination, and a sense of fun**

3 **understanding how to apply intelligent analysis to texts and situations**

4 **being able to demonstrate non-verbal behaviour between people**

5 **knowing how to use your voice effectively in public**

6 **being able to create and maintain a sense of reality in imagined circumstances**

7 **being able to adapt performance style and size to suit the medium**

8 **knowing how to manage and act on criticism**

9 **being willing to actively network with people in the industry**

Let's now look at each of these skills in turn.

1 An ability to achieve a state of full physical and mental relaxation

An important, overarching skill which you will need as an actor is the ability to relax physically and mentally under pressure. Relaxation is important for a number of reasons. Firstly, and most obviously, you will need to be able to feel confident under stressful circumstances (of which there are many – starting with auditions). Secondly, the ability to selectively relax muscles will help you overcome tension-related barriers to effective performance, such as tension in the throat (which harms the voice). Thirdly (this sounds a bit artsy but stay with it), the state of being fully physically and mentally relaxed can be used as an effective meditative state from which to build a mental and physical profile which is appropriate to the character you're playing. Put simply, you can stop being too locked into being 'you', make yourself a sort of blank canvas, and create your character from there.

Fortunately, physical relaxation is a skill which is relatively easy to develop with practice. But you will need a good teacher or at the very least a partner who can help you spot the difference between 'relaxed' and 'slightly tensed'. Ideally you will be a student, or a prospective student, on a reputable training course for performers. If you're not currently training there's a good chance that some kind of initial relaxation training is available near you: all cities and most towns have appropriate evening or day classes in physical relaxation, although it's likely to come under a more impressive banner such as yoga or stress management. Do your research: the key to effective physical relaxation is to regularly work on isolating, tensing and relaxing the various muscles of the body until you can do so at will. This takes practice.

If you can't make it to a good weekly class, or you do your research and can't find one, you could try teaching yourself to relax using one of the recorded relaxation guides available on the market. Indeed I would advise that you use both class and guide, as you need to spend time teaching yourself to relax and that's not always easy in a room full of other students. The best relaxation guides are positive in tone and are carefully-paced to allow you to imagine that the teacher is actually there with you.

Some relaxation guides are more to do with therapy than relaxation. If you can, 'audition' them first. What you need is a calm, controlled, step-by-step recording of how to take yourself through staged relaxation, spoken by someone whose voice you feel able to trust. There are some words in the Appendix (Relaxation Exercise with Visualisation) which you might like to learn and use. You could even record the words yourself and play them back as you relax. Practise every day: it will definitely help you in your everyday life.

So much for physical relaxation. What about mental stress? The mental challenges of being an actor are well-documented – from the pressure to recall lines in public to the confidence-sapping experience of being judged and often rejected on the basis of simply how you look. What can you do to cope with such pressure? One solution, which has come to actors partly via sports psychology, is to use visualisation – meaning, controlled use of the imagination to build a sense of confidence and self-belief. A golfer will imagine sweetly putting the ball from the edge of the green; the actor can imagine in detail any number of positive outcomes, from playing an upcoming scene with skill and truth, to hearing their agent phone to say, 'You've got the part'. Since actors rely on energetic use of the imagination as a central tool in their job, it should come easier for them than for most. But, again, active imagining needs practice.

2 An ability to work creatively with stamina, determination, and a sense of fun

Actors are hardly unique in requiring these qualities in the world of work. But acting is a job which is full of contradictions, and these carry their own pressures. You will need stamina to cope with the long hours in the rehearsal room or on set; much of your time will be spent waiting your turn to rehearse or record (I waited a full three days to shoot anything on my first film). And when the call comes you must be totally ready for action.

There are plenty of banana skins to slip on, even if you're being treated well – last-minute script or schedule changes, technical hitches, a sudden loss of confidence or health, fellow actors who annoyingly save their 'real' performance for the camera or the stage. So you have to stay focused on the job, listen to the people who need you to listen, and be determined to acquit yourself well. You can do some obvious things to help yourself: keep healthy; try to sleep well; and work on your ability to keep energy in reserve by using mental and physical relaxation techniques. Many actors have a relaxing solo hobby which they carry around with them: reading, sketching, writing, doing crosswords. Learn to tick over: if you rev up too much you'll eventually run out of fuel. But you can't afford to switch your engine off completely; leave the engine on and put yourself in neutral.

Determination is an essential quality for any actor. Modern acting is not really, I'm afraid, pure art – when you boil it all down it's first and foremost a commercial service. You do a job for an agreed fee during specified hours. If the artistic muse doesn't arrive – well, you'll just have to act anyway. And then at the next audition you're either right for the part or you're not. If not, you will still be unemployed. After a run of knock-backs at auditions you'll feel like giving up.

Don't. Be determined, be patient, and hunt out the next audition. It's occasionally overlooked during training that an actor is a business. You offer your appearance and your ability to act to schedule, and you do so in an overcrowded market. If you don't have an agent, you must find your own work. If you do have an agent, some of the time you will still have to find your own work. You need to be determined.

This all sounds very serious and of course it is. So where's the fun in being an actor? It's there, and you need to find it and embrace it. You can help yourself maintain a positive creative working attitude whether in or out of work by remaining 'playful'. Professional actors are paid to act because people consider them to be really good at sharing the things in their imagination. However serious and committed you become as an actor, you will always be imagining, playing. That's why, at heart, acting is tremendous fun. It must be – it's a passionate hobby for millions of amateurs worldwide. So don't take yourself too seriously. And don't hold up a shoot or a rehearsal to make a serious point, unless you're certain the director will want to hear it. Keep a sense of perspective and keep a sense of fun.

3 An ability to apply intelligent analysis to texts or situations

Again, there are no unique skills required for an actor to assess and understand a text or situation, and a good director will have strategies in hand to help the actors learn important things about the context of a play. The planning stage is crucial. Section Two of this book explores one method for preparing for rehearsal and performance. At the start of the rehearsal stage in theatre there may well be some brief discussion on matters such as the playwright's intention, the personal histories of key characters and the presence of subtext. Such discussions can be very helpful in guiding the actor towards creating the world of the play in their own imagination. But time is precious in the business, and, as rehearsal periods shrink further and further, so must all discussion be seen to serve the task of communicating the play to the audience. These days it's mostly up to the actor to analyse their script and research the world around the play. The more remote the piece is from the actor's own world, the more important it is to conduct high-quality research, and to come to some agreement with director and other actors regarding the world these characters inhabit. Everything from politics, culture, food, history, social and sexual mores, religion, economic circumstances, climate, class structure, and time of year is fair game for the actor's microscope.

4 An ability to demonstrate non-verbal behaviour between people

An understanding of, and ability to demonstrate, physical behaviour will be central to your task of communicating effectively to an audience. Accordingly, a complete Section is dedicated to the development of these practical skills.

5 An ability to use the voice effectively in public

Public speaking topped both spiders and even *death* in a recent survey of people's greatest phobias. Yet public speaking is central to virtually any acting performance. So how do actors cope? Once again relaxation technique is important along with a focused, positive state of mind. There are some excellent and highly specialised practical handbooks available, which can help the actor become confident and competent in the effective development of vocal technique (see Further Reading in the Appendix). Practice in rehearsal and performance is obviously essential. High quality technical vocal training will leave you feeling confident in voice use onstage and on set, and the best way to develop this is undoubtedly to work with a good voice coach, backing this up with a good book or two. Once this confidence and competence is in place you'll feel able to use and vary such characteristics as tone, inflection, note, loudness, pace, accent and diction. We will explore these aspects of voice and speech, along with some basics on voice use, in Sections Four and Five.

6 An ability to create and maintain a sense of reality in imagined circumstances

Actors basically pretend. They pretend to be other people in circumstances imagined by a writer. If the actor concentrates really hard on the pretence, and the writing is good, the audience will probably be drawn in and invest belief in the situations portrayed on the stage, and the story can be told.

But what can you do to pretend so convincingly that you really start to believe? Smart actors will use everything around them onstage to partially 'trick' themselves into believing that they are a character in a real situation, rather than just an actor in a show. Set, costume, props, and mood created through lighting are all visual stimuli which can help an actor to believe in the situation onstage. Sound, too, can be a valuable stimulus to belief.

A lot of what you're required to do as an actor is crazy when you think about it. As a professional actor I've been, variously, an astronaut who has his heart torn out by an alien; a businessman who is zapped onto the hard drive of a computer; a psychotic armed robber who terrorises pubgoers; and a litter-bug comedy cop who is chased down a street by a gang of schoolchildren. At drama school my teachers didn't do a 'How to react to having your heart ripped from your chest' workshop, but they did help me rediscover the sheer pleasure of playing games. An actor is paid to take risks, to take characters into those exciting areas that normal people tend to avoid at all costs. The call of duty might require you to strip naked, be really ugly, kiss strangers (of both genders), stand screaming on top of a mountain, weep in a crowded room (perhaps even all at once). Such madness needs practice, unless you're mad already. So practise actively imagining things and practise remembering things from your past. Practise re-experiencing things, so that you're not afraid of calling on memories and sensations from your own life. Exercise your imagination as if it is a muscle because, like a muscle, it'll strengthen with repeated use. And improvise – practise the exhilarating craft of making things up without a script. Get together with a few acting students who are trusted friends, meet somewhere safe, and dare to have fun. And read on: the final Section of this book, entitled Inner Life, explores in more detail how to harness your imagination.

Spontaneity in performance is obviously central to being believed. Some people can create a sense of spontaneity at will, others can't. And those who can't won't ever be convincing actors. Maintaining spontaneity with repetition is not easy – yet this is what television and film routinely demand. Staying spontaneous during a three-show theatre run is not too difficult because the adrenalin rush keeps you sharp. But what happens when the nerves wear off or when the pattern of an actor's performance – stage movement, vocal inflection, pacing and so on – becomes fixed through repetition? An actor who has been performing the same role for several weeks, or even months, must find ways to keep their performance fresh each time. Again, we will be looking at ways to retain spontaneity later in the book.

7 An ability to adapt performance style and size to suit the medium

Within live theatre, one of the more difficult skills you will need to develop is the ability to 'turn up' or 'bring down' the level of your performance in response to the needs of the venue or the medium. Ultimately this is all about clear communication – trying to work out what your audience needs, and giving it to them. How you go about it depends on the type of play you're in – it can be easier, for instance, if you're in a play where you speak directly to the audience, and can gauge their reactions. It's worth considering, then, which type of actor you instinctively tend to be; it can give you confidence in your strengths, and can help you identify areas for development (see p. xv). Key issues around performing in different spaces are explored in the final Section, 'Acting in Space'.

8 An ability to manage and act on criticism

Throughout their working lives, actors receive criticism which is often pretty direct and personal. And it can hurt. It is, after all, undeniably you who is being criticised: your talent, your looks, your voice, your age, your range, your intellect, even your sense of confidence. Even a playwright can rationalise criticism of their work by thinking of it as a play, a script, something they created which is now over there on that stage, altered by others. For the actor, the finger points straight at him: the thing being criticised is the same thing that goes home after the show and climbs into bed. So actors may as well get used to it coming their way and try to manage it. Managing it means interpreting it and doing some-thing useful with it. (My first national newspaper review labeled my West End debut as 'charismatic'. My then agent read it and said, 'We don't see it, Paul'. I use the first bit of criticism as a con-fidence boost and I chuckle about the second. What else can I do?)

After an audition, a professional actor might reasonably expect some useful and honest feedback. For practical reasons – most of all, pressure of time – they almost never get it. A much better source for useful critical feedback is in a workshop, such as those run at student drama festivals. You'll often find yourself working with experienced professionals who, because they are being paid simply to run workshops, will answer your questions honestly. You'll gain practice at your craft, and you might even make a useful contact.

9 A willingness to network with people in the industry

There isn't space in a book on acting skills to explore this quality in any detail, but it is an absolutely crucial one. Any business which offers a new product to the market will sensibly focus a lot of time and energy on promotion and advertising. An actor is no different, except that the potential buyer of an actor's services is already awash with alternatives which are tried, tested and trusted, and they don't like you cold-calling one bit!

There is good advice out there for any actor who wants to reach potential employers (see Further Reading) and of course for a trained actor it typically starts with a professional-quality self-introduction via an emailed CV and photo. If you're going to launch yourself as a professional actor but you don't have an agent to make the introductions for you – bad luck. You'll have to get writing away. If you do land an agent – well, good – but don't expect them to get you too much in the way of auditions, though a good agent will also be able to fix up informal (and hugely valuable) chats with casting directors. Some actors offer showreels on DVD, others have their own websites. All actors are likely to have a presence in an appropriate casting directory. In acting, visibility is all: you've got to try to be at the top of the pile of photos and not in the bottom drawer, or in the trash.

A professional actor will normally meet casting directors and directors on their 'home turf', and in such situations the actor is steered through the process on their terms, which can leave little opportunity to make a lasting impression. A brave actor will seek out those rare moments where directors, casting directors and agents come out of their bunkers and face the great unwashed of the acting profession present and future – the workshops, the visits to see a show, the talks to students. If you do launch yourself as an actor and you find yourself next to them in the bar, say hello. Be genuine, friendly, but not overbearing. And shock them by asking them about themselves. Shock them even more by listening and there's a chance they'll remember you!

This Section looks at the planning stage of acting. Actors need to plan for acting so that they can set to work rehearsing with confidence, knowing that they understand the story and the context of the play, the likely personality of their own character, and the nature of key relationships within the play.

To enable you to plan effectively, this Section will show you how to use **three key planning Tools**.

Tool Number 1 is the Character Profile Sheet. This is a 'collecting point' for all the research you carry out when you are reading and re-reading the play prior to, and during, rehearsal. You'll be shown how each category listed on the Character Profile Sheet contributes to your understanding of the character, of the play and of key relationships.

Tool Number 2 shows you how Setting the Status enables you to further explore relationships with insight and confidence.

Tool Number 3 addresses how Power Matters in understanding why key characters allow others to behave the way they do.

At the end of our analysis of each of the Tools you will, within the next four Sections of the book, be offered Acting Tips, along with Solo and Partnered Exercises. Where appropriate we will also refer to published playscripts, and at times to one script in particular – Anton Chekhov's *Three Sisters*. In the Appendix of this book you'll find a completed Character Profile Sheet for the character of Natasha from *Three Sisters*. As this book progresses we will refer to Natasha, and to scenes involving Natasha (in the chronological order in which they occur), to consider how various Tools might be used in performance.

Tool No. 1: The Character Profile Sheet

What do you usually do before you get to work on learning lines and rehearsing? Picture the scene: you hold the script in your hand for the first time and – what? Count your lines? Colour them in with a highlighter pen? Read your lines aloud to 'hear' your character speak for the first time? Start learning the lines straight off? All very tempting (and I'll admit to having done all of the above at some point). But if you want to create a real, believable, three-dimensional character *who belongs in the same script and story as the other characters* – you'll need to do some planning first.

At the back of this book in the Appendix you'll find a blank **Character Profile Sheet**. This is a single-page document, a copy of which you should begin to complete in pencil when you start work on creating a new character. In the Appendix you'll also find **Guidelines on how to complete the Character Profile Sheet**. There's also a completed Character Profile Sheet – the one created for Natasha in Chekhov's *Three Sisters* – which is offered partly as an example of how the completed version might look. The idea is that, before rehearsals begin, you have a single place to pull together the discoveries you make as you read and re-read the script.

As rehearsals begin, each actor's sheet can be altered and added to as new discoveries take place. The sheet also acts as a focus for discussion, so that two actors can discuss, say, conflicts between their characters by referring to their own research. This sort of work is always useful in helping to keep actors in the same play.

Each of the areas which we will explore in this Section has a matching area on the Character Profile Sheet. When you've worked through this Section, have a go at completing a Character Profile Sheet on yourself – the character of You. It's quite sobering to stand back after completing such a sheet to reflect on how you came to be who you are, as a result of the some of the things explored below.

Unearthing the clues: start with the facts

After the first reading of the play what do you already know about your character? Some playwrights are more generous than others in supplying background information on your character's life, some prefer to be vague but many facts are obvious anyway. Roughly how old is the character? What family do you know of? What's the character's occupation and what did they do before that? Where do they live? What events have taken place in their life before the play begins? These are pure facts and these facts help to give you a clear starting point from which to get to know the character. Add them to your Character Profile Sheet in the **FACTS** section. Don't be tempted to ignore any of these facts – the playwright has put them there for a reason, and if you want your character to remain in the same story as the others, nothing should be ignored. Once you start comparing your character's facts with the facts about other characters, you will start to see how the jigsaw of the play fits together.

Example: Natasha from *Three Sisters*

From the playscript we can deduce the following about Natasha:

- she is a local girl
- during the story she is engaged to, then marries, Andrei
- she marries above her social class
- she gains wealth through marriage
- she runs the house once she is married
- she becomes mother to Sophie and Bobik

- her husband is a gambler and a would-be academic
- she learns to speak some French
- she believes servants should be sacked when they are too old to work well
- she begins an affair with Protopopov

History matters

❝ ... other people, friends, family, sociologists, the media, they're the ones who tell us who we are. I mean, let's face it, if tomorrow you or I lost everyone around us, we'd instantly become sort of non-people, wouldn't we? ❞

Alex in Virtual Reality *by Alan Ayckbourn*

A person's sense of identity is strongly influenced by other people. It seems a fair bet that if you've spent the best part of your life being told you're stupid by everyone around you, then you're unlikely to pursue a career in astrophysics. On the other hand, if others have convinced you over time that you're really quite a witty person, then chances are you'll wear this label like a sheriff's badge and will be as witty as you can at every turn. Nicknames are labels too and labels which describe an attitude or behaviour are particularly hard to shake off: 'lazy bones', 'moan-a-lot', 'Lord Snooty' – imagine how it might affect you to be branded with one of these names day in, day out. Academic psychologists refer to this as 'stereotype threat' – a useful term that I'd say captures the essence of the problem for some.

Experience matters too. Successes and failures in life cast long shadows. If you did badly in important school exams then, whatever the cause, you'll probably still in later years wear a label which says, 'No Good At Exams'. By the time you reach adulthood you have countless labels from parents, peers, pedagogues and partners – so many that it would be hard indeed to sum up who 'you' are in a single phrase. Of course, the only labels that really affect your sense of self are the ones of which you're aware.

If the polite next-door neighbour secretly thinks you're a boring and self-obsessed acting student – but they never actually tell you – then you may go on 'fascinating' them with theatrical anecdotes for years to come.

What's true for people in life is also true for characters in plays. A good playwright or scriptwriter may well weave in labels which are there to be unpicked. As a committed transformational character actor you should rise to the challenge: winkle them out, line them up, and decide how much they matter to the characters. When you've done this, add them to the **'What you have heard others say about you'** section of the Character Profile Sheet. Now you can start to look with more confidence through the eyes of your character. One word of warning though. A famous classical actor did something like this once when working on a play. After collecting a sizeable bunch of quotes from other characters, he mentioned his research to his director – also the playwright – who frowned, then observed, 'Well, of course, they could all be lying'.

Example: Natasha from *Three Sisters*

People say the following things in front of Natasha:

- 'I love you – I want you to be my wife' (Andrei)
- 'You're so young, so beautiful, so wonderful!' (Andrei)
- 'You were so rude to Nanny just now' (Olga)
- 'The way she's going around you'd think it was her who started the fire' (Masha)

Things Natasha may have overheard:

- 'It isn't Bobik that's sick, it's her up there ... stupid woman!' (Masha)
- 'The way she dresses – it's absolutely pitiful! And her cheeks shining, absolutely scrubbed!' (Masha)

A question of personality

How would you describe your character's personality? For that matter, how would you describe your own personality? A well-written character will, like you, be full of interesting patterns and contradictions. Some super-confident stage actors can turn out to be very shy. Apparently calm people can suddenly become really aggressive. Born leaders can lose all confidence in themselves. This is true in life as in drama. Totally predictable people are the least interesting people; totally predictable characters in plays are the least interesting characters.

Imagine you're cast as an English vicar in a play. How would you describe the personality of the vicar? The stereotypical English vicar in modern drama will always be well-meaning, helpful, easily embarrassed, possibly a slight stutterer. That's what the audience is probably expecting when you walk onstage, or enter onscreen, wearing your dog-collar. So far so predictable; and in a comedy built around stereotypes, this may well be just what the writer intends (and what the audience wants). But what if it's not a comedy of stereotypes? What if the playwright intends a character who is more 'real'?

The temptation is often to do the opposite, even if it's not really in the play. For example:

Give the vicar a crisis of faith; make them rude, unhelpful – perhaps an alcoholic? Anything, in fact, to make them interesting.

Resist. Trust the playwright. Look for new clues to the character's real personality. And remember that a person's job doesn't necessarily define them. My village's local vicar was formerly a policeman and was later to become a hugely successful children's author.

Read the script afresh and run a personality assessment of your character. I use part of a personality test which has been used in the 'real world', one which was created by the late Professor Hans Eysenck (see Further Reading). It allows you to identify the full range of behaviours and attitudes shown by your character throughout the play, and it lets you see what your character's predominant personality tends to be, so that you might, for instance, conclude that your character is a stable introvert or a neurotic extrovert. It works as a way of assessing the whole personality. The test is below the title word **Personality** on the blank Character Profile Sheet in the Appendix.

Example: Natasha from *Three Sisters*

Natasha is something of an outsider to the three sisters and the servants, coming, as she does, from a lower social class and from the local area. She marries a man who gambles and is unhappy in his career, and she takes on an unfamiliar role as effective head of the running of the house. We see her fretting about her children, and we glean that she eventually starts an affair. Under these circumstances her behaviour in the scenes within the play reveals much edginess and insecurity. Looking at the left-hand side of the 'Personality' section on the Character Profile Sheet, there seems little evidence of stable behaviour, other that she can at times be talkative. In contrast most of the categories on the right-hand side seem to apply: she is by turns impulsive and aggressive (e.g. when turning on the servant Anfisa for daring to sit down in her presence); rigid (e.g. insisting on taking Irina's room from her); anxious (e.g. over her children's health); unsociable (e.g. cancelling the entertainers). As an actor preparing to play Natasha, you have reason to think of her as quite a neurotic person – perhaps a little more extrovert than introvert, but neurotic nonetheless. Such an analysis of a character's personality can be a warning to you. If you play her simply as a neurotic type, you run the risk of being predictable. So look too for the warmth and stability in her, even if it is only somewhere in the background.

Tool No. 2: Setting the Status

Keith Johnstone writes of the 'seesaw principle', whereby a person's sense of status (I think of it as their sense of importance in relation to others) is strongly affected by the physical behaviour of someone else. I go down, you go up; you go down, I go up.

> Walk into a dressing room and say 'I got the part' and everyone will congratulate you, but will feel lowered. Say 'They said I was too old' and people commiserate, but cheer up perceptively.
>
> *Keith Johnstone, writing in* Impro

Johnstone briliantly exposes how we all, consciously and subconsciously, play status games all the time. He offers valuable lessons for the actor in how to develop better status-playing skills.

There are three distinct but related types of status, which we all use: **social**, **verbal** and **physical**. The first is the type over which we have least control: **social status**.

Social status

Social status attaches to you as a result of how society views people in your position. There is a pecking order in society which dictates that a king is more important than a homeless person and that a bank manager has higher social status than an office cleaner. It's important to be aware of social status before you play around with the other two types because your 'normal' social status is always lurking there in the background when people interact with you. Next time you're in a room full of strangers, imagine that one of them is a rich and successful rock musician who is hoping to avoid being spotted. You can almost see the glow around them as they begin to stand out from the ordinary mortals.

Social status has much to do with power. The more power you have to influence others, the higher up the social hierarchy you'll go. Rock stars have incredible power when they are successful, but once they stop selling their music they are on a steep and slippery slope.

It's useful to know about social status because conflict in plays often comes from a character losing, or gaining, social status. King Lear's steady loss of social status is at the heart of his tragedy. In *A Midsummer Night's Dream*, Bottom's hike in social status among the fairy people, despite his having sprouted the head of an ass, is at the heart of that comedy. Films make the switch often: the old Eddie Murphy/Dan Ackroyd hit comedy *Trading Places* is perhaps one of the best known.

Play study: The Admirable Crichton *by J M Barrie*

J.M. Barrie's inspired play *The Admirable Crichton*, written in the early twentieth century, takes the comedy and the drama of social status 'switching' to its highest level. His play maroons an upper-class English family on a desert island, and places them at the mercy of their ever-resourceful butler.

Act One sees Ernest summoning the servants 'upstairs' for tea with his aristocratic friends. Before long, the party is in full and unbearably awkward swing, with Crichton's fellow (subordinate) servants being forced to attempt polite conversation with Ernest's upper class friends. The emerging nub of Barrie's play is raised in conversation between Crichton and Lord Loam:

LORD LOAM
Can't you see, Crichton, that our divisions into classes are artificial, that if we were to return to nature, which is the aspiration of my life, all would be equal?

CRICHTON
If I may make so bold as to contradict your lordship –

LORD LOAM *(with an effort)*
Go on.

CRICHTON

> The divisions into classes, my lord, are not artificial. They
> are the natural outcome of a civilised society. *(To LADY
> MARY)* There must always be a master and servants in all
> civilised communities, my lady, for it is natural, and what-
> ever is natural is right.

Act Two begins following shipwreck, as the truth of Crichton's
belief is put to the test. Ernest, selected friends and servants
struggle to adapt to desert island living. Butler Crichton's
resourcefulness and energy quickly bring him status and
authority as he sets about building a home for the party; meanwhile Ernest sits uselessly on an upturned bucket and composes
verse. But not for long:

CRICHTON *(to LADY MARY)*

> ... until a ship comes we are three men who are going to do
> our best for you ladies.

LADY MARY *(with a curl of the lip)*

> Mr. Ernest does no work.

CRICHTON *(cheerily)*

> But he will, my lady.

LADY MARY

> I doubt it.

CRICHTON *(confidently, but perhaps thoughtlessly)*

> No work – no dinner – will make a great change in Mr.
> Ernest.

LADY MARY

> No work – no dinner. When did you invent that rule,
> Crichton?

CRICHTON *(loaded with bamboo)*
> I didn't invent it, my lady. I seem to see it growing all over the island ...

Act Three – entitled 'The Happy Home' – brings us up to date with events of the previous two years, which have seen Crichton emerge as the unchallenged leader of the group, a man who has built a home bursting with desert island luxuries. We learn that, indeed, everyone is changed; Lady Mary has become a huntress, and even Ernest now pulls his weight, albeit under threat of 'the bucket', a water punishment which his former butler imposes when deemed necessary. Crichton, now known to all as 'The Gov.', turns his full force on the adoring Lady Mary:

CRICHTON
> I am lord over all. They are but hewers of wood and drawers of water for me. These shores are mine. Why should I hesitate; I have no longer any doubt. I do believe I am doing the right thing. Dear Polly, I have grown to love you; are you afraid to mate with me? *(She rocks her arms; no words will come from her.)* 'I was a king in Babylon, And you were a Christian slave.'

LADY MARY *(bewitched)*
> You are the most wonderful man I have ever known, and I am not afraid ...

But as they all dance to celebrate the forthcoming union between 'The Gov.' and Lady Mary, a shot signals the arrival of a rescue party of English sailors.

Within moments, the natural order of things starts to melt back to old ways.

Act Four returns us to 'the other island' – England. Ernest has penned a shockingly untruthful revision of events on the desert island, in which he positions himself as hero and provider – a version which is supported heartily by his aristocratic fellow-adventurers. In this version Crichton plays only a small supporting role as the reliable butler. Yet Crichton seems happy to play along with the deception. The play ends with this private exchange between Crichton and Lady Mary:

LADY MARY

Do you despise me, Crichton? *(The man who could never tell a lie makes no answer.)* You are the best man among us.

CRICHTON

On an island, my lady, perhaps; but in England, no.

LADY MARY

Then there's something wrong with England.

CRICHTON

My lady, not even from you can I listen to a word against England.

LADY MARY

Tell me one thing: you have not lost your courage?

CRICHTON

No, my lady.

(She goes. He turns out the lights.)

So ends one of the greatest social status 'switch' comedies of all time – with a warning, perhaps, to the audience of the time to look to their own conscience and prejudices.

A feature of social status switching is, of course, that characters react to changing circumstances by altering what they say and what they do. What they say, we can call their **verbal status**; what they do, we can call their **physical status**.

Verbal status

Every spoken word or phrase carries with it a status. The speaker's words, and the attitude behind those words, automatically claim a position for the speaker on the status seesaw. If the two people on the seesaw have opposite social status – a king and a cleaner for example – then the stage is set for verbal status activity which undermines the established relative social status. The most obvious way to use verbal status to claim top spot on the seesaw is to insult someone horribly and sound as if you really mean it. The more unpleasant the image you can create in people's minds, the lower you're forcing the person being insulted. Helena and Hermia's furious barrage of insults aimed at one another's height in Shakespeare's *A Midsummer Night's Dream*, stands as a good example. I've marked the verbal status insults in bold; as you'll see the seesaw hammers up and down as speedily as the audience can follow it:

HELENA

...What, will you tear impatient answers from my gentle tongue?

Fie, fie, you **counterfeit**, you **puppet** you!

HERMIA

Puppet? Why so? Ay that way goes the game.

Now I perceive that she hath made compare

Between our statures. She hath urged her height,

And with her personage – her tall personage –

Her height, forsooth – she hath prevailed with him.

– And are you grown so high in his esteem

Because **I am so dwarfish** and so **low**?

How low am I thou **painted maypole**? Speak

How low am I? I am not yet so low

But that my nails can reach unto thine eyes.

HELENA

> I pray you though you mock me gentlemen,
> Let her not hurt me. I was never curst,
> **I have no gift at all in shrewishness –**
> I am a right maid for my cowardice.
> Let her not strike me. You perhaps may think
> Because **she is something lower than myself**
> That I can match her...

Followed a few lines later with –

HELENA

> O when she's angry **she is keen and shrewd.**
> **She was a vixen** when she went to school
> And **though she is but little she is fierce.**

HERMIA

> Little again! Nothing but low and little!
> Why will you suffer her to flout me thus?
> Let me come to her...

At which point Lysander joins in with –

LYSANDER

> Get you gone you **dwarf**!
> You **minimus of hind'ring knot-grass made**!
> You **bead**! you **acorn**!

A Midsummer Night's Dream, Act 3 Scene 2

It follows that the easiest way to offer someone else top spot on the seesaw is to compliment them, and do it as sincerely as you can. In Shakespeare's *King Richard III*, the Duke of Gloucester (later King Richard III) plays this trick to the hilt in his seduction of Lady Anne, whose husband he has just killed. She's just spat at him for claiming he would be a better husband to her than her beloved Edward:

GLOUCESTER

Why dost thou spit at me?

ANNE

Would it were mortal poison, for thy sake!

GLOUCESTER

Never came poison from so sweet a place.

ANNE

Never hung poison on a fouler toad.
Out of my sight! Thou dost infect my eyes.

GLOUCESTER

Thine eyes, sweet lady, have infected mine.

ANNE

Would they were basilisks, to strike thee dead!

GLOUCESTER

I would they were, that I might die at once;
For now they kill me with a living death...

King Richard III, Act 1 Scene 2

Add a believable criticism of yourself, so lowering your own status, and you confirm your partner's unassailable place as 'top dog'. Some sixteen lines later Anne hears this from the future King:

GLOUCESTER

I never sued to friend nor enemy;
My tongue could never learn sweet smoothing words;
But, now thy beauty is proposed my fee, My proud heart
sues and prompts my tongue to speak.

They marry shortly afterwards! Of course it's not usually straight-forward. In our modern society, extreme insults and unfettered compliments are regarded with distaste in almost equal measure. Insults, if sincere, are so status-lowering that they can lead to physical violence (think of football hooligans); extreme compliments lead straight to suspicion as to the speaker's motives. We humans are though generally pretty sophisticated, so we use tricks and techniques to negotiate a position for ourselves on each new seesaw we sit on with each new partner.

Followers of a theory named **Transactional Analysis** define all our verbal status behaviour as falling into one of three types: **adult, parent** or **child**. Whenever we speak, it's said, we unconsciously select one of these roles to make our point. And we often choose a role which is contrary to our social status. Reality TV shows love this theme: the 'bad' mother who rules her children by throwing tantrums, celebrities who behave like spoilt teenagers after downing a few drinks. But the social status switch can also be intentional. The primary school teacher who asks a small child to help solve an equation is using child-to-parent behaviour: the teacher secretly knows the answer, but raises the child's place on the seesaw in order to give the child the confidence to have a go at the problem. Of course you'd have to hear the conversation to be sure: a sarcastic tone from the teacher, for example, would plunge the child back down by implying that they were not worthy of real respect. The insult in such a case is hidden in the tone of the voice rather than in the actual words.

Transactional Analysis is a useful way in to understanding verbal status. For a masterclass in the use of adult/parent/child verbal status, we can turn to Alan Ayckbourn's poignant and brilliantly observed *Mother Figure*. In this play, one of the *Confusions* series of five interlinked plays, a bullying husband is brought to a standstill by the controlling parent-to-child behaviour of his neighbour, a desperately isolated young mother.

Play study: Mother Figure *by Alan Ayckbourn*

This one-act play takes place in the sitting room of Lucy, a stressed and permanently dressing-gowned mother of small children. Neighbour Rosemary imposes herself to deliver a phone message from Lucy's absentee husband. But Lucy has descended so far into a world dominated by the needs of small children that she seems unable to manage 'proper' adult-to-adult interaction:

LUCY

Would you like a drink or something?

ROSEMARY

A drink? Oh – well – what's the time? Well – I don't know if I should. Half past – oh yes, well – why not? Yes, please. Why not? A little one.

LUCY

Orange or lemon?

ROSEMARY

I beg your pardon?

LUCY

Orange juice or lemon juice? Or you can have milk.

ROSEMARY

Oh, I see. I thought you meant ...

LUCY

Come on. Orange or lemon? I'm waiting ...

ROSEMARY

Is there a possibility of some coffee?

LUCY

No.

ROSEMARY

Oh.

LUCY

It'll keep you awake. I'll get you an orange, it's better for you.

ROSEMARY

Oh.

LUCY *(as she goes)*

Sit still. Don't run around. I won't be a minute.

So begins a wonderfully relentless sequence in which Lucy stays locked into a parent-to-child mode of verbal status behaviour. Even the arrival of Terry, Rosemary's controlling husband, fails to snap Lucy out of it. Terry draws his wife into an awkward argument about the role of men and women in the home, and they are both told off by Lucy, who then goes to fetch a drink for Terry (a glass of milk). While Lucy is out of the room Terry too slips into parent-child mode – aggressively this time – as he has 'words' with his wife:

TERRY

... we'll have less of that, too, if you don't mind.

ROSEMARY

What?

TERRY

All this business about me never going out of the house.

ROSEMARY

It's true.

TERRY

And even if it is true, you have no business saying it in front of other people.

ROSEMARY

Oh, honestly, Terry, you're so touchy. I can't say a thing
right these days can I?

TERRY

Very little. Now you come to mention it.

The conversation takes a downward turn as, nursing her glass of
orange juice, Rosemary launches an attack on a biscuit-
munching Terry which pulls them both into child-to-child mode:

ROSEMARY

Niggle, niggle, niggle. You keep on at me the whole time.
I'm frightened to open my mouth these days. I don't know
what's got into you lately. You're in a filthy mood from the
moment you get up till you go to bed ...

TERRY

What are you talking about?

ROSEMARY

Grumbling and moaning ...

TERRY

Oh, shut up.

ROSEMARY

You're a misery to live with these days, you really are.

TERRY

I said, shut up.

Terry snatches his wife's juice and finishes it, reducing her to
tears. Lucy strides in and tells Terry off: he, in a sulk, is forced to
apologise and then to drink his milk. At the end of the play the
married neighbours are reconciled and leave the house together:

LUCY
> All right. Off you go, both of you.

ROSEMARY *(kissing her on the cheek)*
> Night night.

LUCY
> Night, night dear. Night, night Terry.

TERRY *(kissing LUCY likewise)*
> Night night.

LUCY
> Sleep tight.

TERRY
> Hope the bed bugs don't bite.

LUCY
> Hold Rosemary's hand, Terry.

> *ROSEMARY and TERRY hold hands*

> See her home safely.

TERRY
> Night.

ROSEMARY
> Night.

LUCY
> Night night.

> *TERRY and ROSEMARY go off hand in hand*

LUCY blows kisses

(with a sigh) Blooming kids. Honestly.

So ends an exhilarating and (when you see it in performance) surprisingly realistic analysis of how 'behaviour breeds behaviour' – with a lesson, perhaps, that if you act like a child then you deserve to be treated like one. Child, parent, adult – the words you use set the tone for the way you develop relationships with those around you.

When you're thinking about how to 'act' verbal status, hold on to the image of a seesaw. There are many more than three potential points of balance on a seesaw and you can modify your respective positions on it by subtly changing the words you use. If you think for a moment how you alter the way you talk to different people in your own life, then you'll surely know what I mean.

Actually, I don't know if you'll know what I mean because we've probably never met. If I'd written, 'you might know what I mean', which is nearer the mark, then you could feel mildly insulted at my implied criticism of your ability to follow my point. If I'd put, 'You'll probably still be totally clueless as to what I'm on about', then the surprise you'd experience on reading these words might lead you to abandon the book entirely (or read on more intently!).

Which brings us (I hope) to an enjoyable complication in the game of verbal status: humour. If we have indeed met – if we are in fact friends – then you won't mind me poking fun at your status as a reader (you can't help struggling with these concepts, can you? Try reading it all again s-l-o-w-l-y.) And you can call my book a heap of turgid, self-indulgent cowdung (probably). Friends allow each other to flout the rules of verbal status, and they use humour as the weapon.

Acting tip

The tantalising thing about all this for an actor is that much of the detail of this stuff can't be known until rehearsal begins. One character fires an insult at another character. Is it a serious insult? Is it a joke which both enjoy? Or is it a clumsy attempt at humour which only one side finds funny? Part of the joy of rehearsal is to find out what's really going on. So come prepared to offer your director, and your fellow-actors, more than one choice of intention to explore.

Exercises: Solo

Solo work on verbal status is, naturally, mostly limited to speech study or scene study. There's some fun and learning to be had, though, by exploring verbal status with people who are unwitting:

1 When you're next in a shop, offer a polite genuine compliment to the assistant on some aspect of their appearance (e.g. their choice of clothing). Watch their reaction carefully as they feel themselves raised on the seesaw.

2 On the next occasion, criticise yourself in some way (e.g. say 'I'm far too fat for this' when trying on a jacket. If they don't comment, add, 'I am, aren't I?'). Note the assistant's reaction.

3 When you next meet an acquaintance (someone who has not read this book!), offer them a huge compliment and at the same time deliver a huge insult to yourself. Note their reaction.

4 When you next meet a really good friend (again, someone who has not read this book), offer them a big insult and at the same time deliver a huge compliment to yourself. Note their reaction – and then tell them what you were doing. (Good luck with the friendship.)

Exercises: Partnered

1 Stand facing your partner. Compliment them for something which you genuinely find impressive – something about their appearance or an aspect of their personality. Begin with the simple phrase, 'Something I really like about you is – '. Your partner now takes a turn and compliments

you. Keep the compliments going, and keep them brief. When you start to run out of things to say, break off and discuss how it felt to receive straightforward compliments.

2 As before. This time insult each other with a comment about the other person's appearance or personality. Don't get too personal! If you're worried that the other person will take serious offence, limit the intensity your insults (e.g. 'you don't always listen properly'). An even less offensive version of this exercise involves using 'gobbledegook' insults – if you tell someone they smell like a dribbetefidgit it somehow feels less offensive. Afterwards, discuss how it felt to receive such insults.

3 As before, but this time offer your partner a barbed compliment which is really a coded insult. You might tell them, 'you do make the best of your hair' or 'you don't look anything like as old as you are' or 'you don't let go when you know you're right about something'. Swap. Discuss how it felt to be on the receiving end.

4 Set up a short 'Master and Servant' improvisation. The servant has to deliver status-lowering insults without the master fully realising what's going on. (A valet helping to choose his master's shoes might ask, 'Sir, would you like the old shoes or the very old shoes?').

5 Conduct a scene-study in which you and a partner identify words and phrases which seem to lower or raise the other person's status. Run the scene with differing intentions. First, perform it with all compliments and insults genuinely felt. Next, perform it as though the two characters are friends having a laugh: this time, all compliments are jokingly insincere and all insults are meant in jest.

In each case, discuss how the activity within each exercise alters the relationship between the two partners or the two characters.

Additional scene for exploring verbal status: *Sucker Punch* by Roy Williams

The following small segment from Williams' hard-hitting play features boxing champion Leon and his former girlfriend Becky. Becky uses words and phrases that are assertive rather than aggressive, though she seems to lower Leon's status during the sequence. A good actor's question might be – to what extent does she mean what she says?

BECKY

You have to stop this, Leon.

LEON

Told you already, girl, I don't know what you're talking about.

BECKY

I know it's you.

LEON

Becks, believe me.

BECKY

Calling me all the time, hanging up when you hear my voice, was annoying.

LEON

Not me.

BECKY

Insulting my boyfriend when he answers the phone, was just plain childish.

LEON

Not me!

BECKY

Now you're stalking me?

LEON

No.

BECKY

This stops now. Are you listening?

LEON

What makes you think it's me?

BECKY

One of my neighbours saw you lurking around earlier. 'Black kid, he looked just like Leon Davidson,' she says.

LEON

Nice!

BECKY

She wanted to call the police. Now she wants an auto-graph. *(Leon chuckles)* Why are you doing this?

LEON

If it was me, did you ever think that maybe it was because I'm looking out for you? It's a rough area you are living in, Becks.

BECKY

I've got Simon looking after me.

LEON

He sounds like a bender.

BECKY

Leon, what is going on in that head?

LEON

   Like I got time to be chasing after you.

BECKY

   This stops, right now.

Physical status

After I've known my acting students for a few weeks I play a trick on them. I call a routine break then return to class. On return I ask the students to sit on the floor and then I pick out individuals in turn, politely inviting their comments on the subject we were working on before the break. As soon as the class gets underway, the students start to tense up. Normally extrovert people begin to lower their heads and hope they won't be picked on to speak. Class jokers stop joking. As I listen to people's faltering comments, bolder individuals catch my eye but quickly look away. Within ten minutes there is silence in the room and a pall of gloom.

   At this point I can bear it no longer and admit to the students that I've been role-playing. I ask them how they've been feeling about me since we came back from the break. Each student was feeling that I was annoyed or upset at them over something. Late arrivals thought they were being cold-shouldered for poor time-keeping; jokers thought I'd found their jokes offensive; speakers had thought they were boring me. I ask them to identify what I'd been doing differently. They tell me I was being aggressive or emotional or unemotional. I ask them not to try to interpret my feelings, but to identify what I had actually been *doing* differently. What was I doing physically that was different from my normal behaviour?

   With questioning and encouragement, the students begin to identify that my physical behaviour had been temporarily altered. Where I would normally have sat at the same level as the group, this time I had stayed standing. I would normally have moved my eye contact around the group, but this time I'd either stared fixedly at an individual or had looked away entirely. I would normally have fidgeted a bit – this time I'd kept very still. These, and other subtle changes in my physical behaviour, had unsettled them and had altered the whole nature of our relationship.

In status terms, I had taken on all the characteristics of high physical status. I'd been physically relaxed but tall; I'd kept my hands on my hips, keeping myself open and so claiming a larger-than-normal physical space; I'd used dominant eye contact, but had offered no supporting behaviour (I didn't nod and smile to encourage speakers to continue). At one or two points I'd moved right up close to individual students, invading their personal space.

You can guess pretty well what signs I would have exhibited if I had been using very low-status physical behaviour. Physical conduct matters hugely in human interaction. In Section Three – The Body – we'll explore this in much more detail. As to exercises, the exploration of physical status is, of course, exploration of body language. The detailed exercises in the next Section will allow you to put these ideas on Physical Status into practice.

When you pull together the three types of status which a person uses – social, verbal and physical – you'll have a pretty sophisticated understanding of that person, and of your feelings towards them. As part of your planning towards acting, it can be useful to represent your status relationship with another character as a sort of a snapshot. And the seesaw image is a particularly strong and simple one to use. In the bottom-right section of the Character Profile Sheet you'll see the title **Status**. Follow the guidelines in the Appendix to show how you can use this section to represent a key status relationship with another character.

Example: Natasha from *Three Sisters*

When you're filling in the seesaw section of a Character Profile Sheet, you're effectively drawing together your sense of your character's overall status – social, verbal and physical – in relation to another key character. Masha makes a useful seesaw partner for Natasha, partly because Masha seems pretty outspoken in her criticism of her brother's wife. When you pull together the facts, the things Natasha has heard Masha say and the snapshot we have of Natasha's personality, it seems likely that Natasha will feel herself strongly inferior to the sophisticated, outspoken Masha. The fact that Natasha is in charge of the running of the house in which Masha lives, becomes, therefore, an interesting complication.

Tool No. 3: Power Matters

The possession of power gives us confidence in dealing with other people. It brings with it status and gives us something definite to negotiate with in everyday life.

Playwrights and actors understand about power – but their knowledge is usually instinctive rather than researched. Power is at the very heart of storytelling. King Lear's tragedy is that of a man who gives away power to people who want more and who in the end take it all from him. The plays of Harold Pinter and Arthur Miller often play explicitly with power, and its uses and abuses, for their central conflicts. But what is power and how can you define it?

Within business training, managers are sometimes taught about power in all its glory, thanks to the work of researchers such as John R. P. French Jr and Bertram Raven. In a section of D. Cartwright and A. Zander's 'Group Dynamics: Research and Theory' (published by Tavistock Publications in 1968) they describe several separately identifiable **types of power**. For me, these boil down to:

1 *Agreed power* – power which a person is allowed to use as a result of their position within a culture (e.g. a manager can ask a junior member of a team to carry out a duty; a police officer is allowed to arrest a suspect; a parent can hold back a child's pocket money as a punishment).

2 *Abuse power* – power which a person uses to force another person to do something (e.g. a school bully threatens

another child unless dinner money is handed over). Abuse power is also used when a person with Agreed power abuses their authority (e.g. a doctor inappropriately asks a patient to strip naked or a police officer strikes a protester during a heated but peaceful protest).

3 *Reward power* – the power to supply something which is valued by another person (e.g. an interviewer rewards a candidate with a job; a parent rewards a child with a sweet; a child rewards a parent with a smile). Crucially, of course, the reward has to be wanted and the more keenly it's wanted the greater is the Reward power held by the power possessor.

4 *Knowledge power* – power which comes from having information or expertise which is needed or wanted by someone else (e.g. a homeless person knows the location of the nearest taxi rank; a technician is able to repair a computer problem; a friend has some juicy gossip).

5 *Connection power* – power which comes from being close to someone who has power (e.g. a school pupil is the daughter of the headmaster; you have a friend who is a famous film actor; an unremarkable acquaintance is the constant companion of someone you find really attractive).

6 *Personal power* – power which comes from a person's attractiveness to others either because of their looks or their personality (e.g. a strikingly beautiful model; a member of a group who can tell jokes brilliantly; someone who is known as a really good listener).

Here's an example of power at work. In this scenario I've marked which power types are being used at each point in the story. There's at least one example of each type of power.

A park keeper sees a homeless male youth sleeping on a park bench in a city centre. The park keeper wakes the youth and orders him to move on (1): the youth gets up and shuffles away. The youth meets a pretty (6) female tourist, an off-duty policewoman, who asks him the way

to the cathedral; they chat, and he gives precise instruc-
tions (4). As they part, the woman offers the youth some
loose change (3): he takes it. The park keeper has been
watching. As the woman starts to leave he goes over to
the youth and demands the money, threatening to report
him for begging (2). The youth calls out to the woman (5),
and she returns and intervenes, showing her warrant card
(1). The park keeper leaves quickly.

A person's power then derives from a variety of sources. Job,
family role, education, skills developed (including for a hobby),
personality, social class – all provide your character with aspects
of power that give them potential influence over others. Films,
plays and television comedies are quite often built around a
central misunderstanding regarding power. Nickolai Gogol's *The
Government Inspector* (1836) stands as a shining example, a play
in which a simple misunderstanding – that a new arrival in town
is an all-important government inspector, when in fact he's
nothing of the sort – leads to a catalogue of incidents and accidents which reveal the darker side of town life. A whole episode
of the classic TV comedy *Fawlty Towers* revolves around the
mistaken belief that a customer is a top restaurant critic. Perhaps
the best movie exploration of mistaken power takes place in the
film *Being There*. An ageing and socially challenged gardener
(Peter Sellers), thrust blinking into the modern world after the
death of his employer, is run over and then nursed by a wealthy
friend of the US President. His social shyness and his randomly
spoken advice on how to help plants grow lead his all-powerful
new friends to adopt him as a brilliant business guru who speaks
in metaphors.

Willy Russell's *Blood Brothers* also takes an overt look at power
– specifically, how access to power gives people advantages in
life. Russell starts with a scenario in which twins from a poor
background are separated at birth. While one twin, Mickey,
remains with his mother – a cleaner – the other, Edward, is
adopted into a wealthy home (where the boys' mother has been

working as a cleaner). We follow the twins' dramatic changes in fortune as they grow up, coming together infrequently so that we (and they) can see the widening gulf between them.

Power issues are often most significant when you are on the receiving end of someone else's power, and Willy Russell offers many examples of how society can favour those who are already advantaged in some way, whether within the fields of education, employment, health or social confidence. Here's an example of how someone with **Agreed power** can choose to apply **Abuse power** (in the form of verbal threats) to one person, and **Reward power** (in the form of friendly advice) to the next. Both twins have been caught red-handed on the point of commiting a petty crime. To Mickey's mother the police officer barks:

> Well, there'll be no more bloody warnings from now on. Either you keep them in order, Missis, or it'll be the courts for you, or worse, won't it?

To Edward's adoptive mother he says:

> An' er, as I say, it was more of a prank really, Mrs Lyons. I'd just dock his pocket money if I was you. *(Laughs)* But one thing I would say, if y'don't mind me sayin', is, well, I'm not sure I'd let him mix with the likes of them in the future. Make sure he keeps with his own kind, Mrs Lyons.

Russell uses the narrative of his musical play to argue persuasively that if we use our various powers to treat people in radically different ways – praising one while chastising the other, favouring one while disadvantaging the other, and so on – then we are, each of us, complicit in influencing the way people turn out.

Acting tips

Once you're aware of the importance of different types of power you can start to use that knowledge to sharpen your sensitivity onstage. As part of the planning stage of acting, you should comb through your script to work out which types of power your character possesses. You can list these for quick reference in the **POWER** section of your Character Profile Sheet.

For actors, awareness of power can really help to clarify why characters behave the way they do and why others allow them to do so. It can also help you to avoid stereotyping. A character with low social status, such as a prostitute, may have an abundance of certain power types: personal (being good-looking); knowledge (of street life and clients' names); connection (with their pimp and with important clients); abuse (threatening to reveal clients' names and preferences); and reward (use your imagination!). Likewise, a character with apparent high social status – the ceremonial mayor of a town, for example – may in truth have very little influence over others.

Exercises: Solo

1 Draw up a list of powers which you personally possess. Be imaginative. If you're unemployed you are still likely to at least have the agreed power to demand payment of benefit within a certain time period. Come up with at least one example per power category of occasions when you've exercised each of these powers over someone else. If you're stuck, identify a power you possess that you might be able to use in the future. (Even 'feeding a pet daily' is an Agreed power.)

2 Think of someone you know well who doesn't strike you as being particularly powerful. List the six power types. Now try to come up with at least one example per power category. (A person's expert knowledge of Star Wars figures might not impress you personally, but...)

3 Select a monologue from a published play that requires you to speak to an onstage character. Comb through the speech for moments when your character seems to be using a specific type of power to influence the other person. Identify the power type being used in each case.

Exercises: Partnered

1 Choose a frozen 'tableau' moment from an imaginary scene in which two power types have momentarily come together in conflict. For example, a parent is about to use Abuse power to strike a child while the child is trying to deflect punishment with Personal power via a friendly pleading expression. Or, a headteacher is trying to use Agreed power to refuse admission to the child of a pushy parent who is offering to write a cheque for school funds. Don't plan the scene, but on a cue unfreeze the action and see what happens. Try removing one of the power bases (e.g. the parent has no spare funds) and see what happens this time. Then try adding some new power to one of the characters.

2 Similar to 1 above. Select a duologue from a published play. Comb through the scene for moments when each character seems to be using a specific type of power to influence the other. Identify the power type being used in each case. Run the scene with a keen awareness of what powers are being used.

3 As above, but this time discuss with your partner some sort of shift in power. For example, if A previously found B very attractive (i.e. B has Personal power), this time B is considered less attractive. Or (taking the imaginary example from 1 above), a parent wanting to use Abuse power against their child is wheelchair-bound. Re-run the scene and discuss how the dynamics have changed, even though the scripted lines remain the same.

Example: Natasha from *Three Sisters*

Chekhov has endowed Natasha with a fascinatingly comprehensive range of powers which, when lined up alongside the powers of Andrei and his sisters, should suggest to us why his play is less a drama of inaction (a common criticism of *Three Sisters*), and more a drama of what powerful people suffer when they find themselves restrained by society and by their own personalities. Natasha is accorded considerable **Agreed power** through her marriage to Andrei – over the servants, for example, and to a lesser degree over her sisters-in-law. She feels justified in sliding over into **Abuse power** at moments where she loses her temper at both servants and sisters. She enjoys her **Reward power** over both Andrei and the children, indulging the latter with comfort (including Irina's room) and attention. As a member of the household she no doubt collects valuable **Information power** over those around her, but her particular expertise seems to derive from her role as a mother (something only she among the four women enjoys). Her **Connection power** to Andrei, and by association to the sisters, brings her status within the local community. And her beauty is a source of **Personal power** over both Andrei and later over Protopopov (no doubt among others). So someone who seems at first reading to be something of an unsophisticated outsider, and perhaps a victim of her own personality, starts to seem altogether more interesting.

section 3: **the body**

In this Section we will be concentrating on how actors, and indeed people in everyday life, use their bodies to communicate things to others. You will be introduced to five new Tools which allow you to change the way you express yourself through the body.

Actors use their knowledge of non-verbal communication to ensure that accurate and appropriate messages reach their audience. When you are onstage or on screen you should be at least partly aware of how your body is communicating things so that you can make adjustments if your communication is somehow wrong. This Section gives you the knowledge you need to achieve such awareness. Actors also use knowledge of physical behaviour to widen their range – i.e. to play a wider cross-section of character types. The five new Tools in this section will help you to become more versatile:

Tool Number 4 – Adjusting Tension – explores how muscle tension reflects a character's psychological state.

Tool Number 5 – Adjusting Height – considers why people alter their height above and below their normal 'standing' height.

Tool Number 6 – Adjusting Openness – examines how, by covering or exposing their chest and stomach, a person can reveal their thoughts and feelings.

Tool Number 7 – Working on Eye Contact – explores the meanings behind differing levels and duration of eye contact.

Tool Number 8 – Adjusting Space – assesses the way we handle physical space when we are with others.

As in the previous Section, you will be given examples, acting tips and exercises to allow you to develop your ability to change your physical behaviour in performance.

At the risk of stating the obvious, no one can actually hear your thoughts. They're yours and if you choose to keep them private you can. People can (and will) guess at what is going on in your mind, but they're only guessing.

Some years ago, a police recruitment poster boasted that officers were trained to spot when a suspect was lying: the suspect would rub their nose when speaking. I imagine quite a few suspects went to court for having an itchy nose.

There are physical signs which even some of our greatest actors can't fake. Sweating, turning pale, going dry in the mouth: these require real psychological stimulus. Beyond these signs, we are as a species pretty good at throwing others off the scent – generally by controlling our animal impulses for fight or flight.

You can still often get a sense of what is really going on in someone's mind. The secret is to keep an eye on what they can't control so well. Broadly speaking, the further away from the face you go, the more revealing the clues are likely to be. A twitch of a finger or foot can say something really important about the mood of a person (experts call a sign such as this twitch 'leakage'). These, and other aspects of the behaviour of the human animal (you could call it the '**humanimal**'), have been comprehensively and fascinatingly explored by experts such as zoologist Desmond Morris (see Further Reading).

For an actor who wants to be really versatile – who wants to portray the widest range of different types of human behaviour – what do you need to know? What are the key variables in the body that alter according to someone's personality and culture? There are five or, at least, four plus a joker in the pack. The variables are **T**ension, **H**eight, **O**penness, **S**pace (or rather use of space) and **E**ye contact; and together they form the mnemonic **THOSE**. Space is the joker, as you'll see.

Tool No. 4: Adjusting Tension

Tension occurs when you contract muscles: they tighten. Often this is for some necessary reason – you want to pick up an object, to move forwards, or simply to avoid falling over. Just standing still demands some muscle tension. Frequently though we use muscles without any such necessary reason. As a result of some psychological stimulus we become tense.

One stereotype of a very tense person is an army regimental sergeant-major. Put in charge of a gang of undisciplined young conscripts, he must knock them into shape in time for inspection by a senior officer. At stake is the reputation both of the regiment and of the sergeant-major as a disciplinarian. He stands ramrod-straight in front of his new charges.

One of the new recruits represents the sergeant-major's biggest challenge and is his opposite in terms of physical tension. This stereotype is a hippy, used to resting and sleeping when and where he feels like it. He is at ease with the world and sees no need to waste energy on pointless drilling. His favourite position is flat on his back, marijuana joint in hand, contemplating the cosmos. The stage is set for conflict ...

Extreme opposites are then easy to recognise, but tension in people normally takes more subtle forms. Among the guests at a showbiz party are two people facing one another. The first, a man, is standing and, although he has no need to move, his body is tense: his brow is knitted, he has slightly lifted shoulders, his stomach is tight, fists and buttocks partially clenched, kneecaps pulled upwards, even his toes are clawed inside his shoes. The woman he speaks to is standing, too, but she uses pretty well only the muscles she needs. There's some tension in her face – she is smiling at the man as he talks – but otherwise her body has only enough tension to allow her to stand and to hold her drink.

In the animal world, tension acts as a state of readiness for fight or flight. The need to be ready to stay and fight, or to suddenly flee, is especially common in animals which are lower down the food chain – i.e. the hunted. Birds and mice are good examples, and they have a metabolism to match: racing heartbeat, sudden, twitchy movements, always on the lookout for trouble. Conversely, the creatures which can relax the most are the ones which are hunted least – i.e. the hunters. Think of lions basking in the sun. They feel no threat so need not be on constant lookout. They use tension only when needed and with economy, perhaps when sauntering to the lake for a drink. Even when hunting at full speed, much of the lion's body is untensed.

In humanimals, mental state is likely to be the biggest factor in determining how tense or how relaxed a person is. Confidence develops, or fails to develop, partly in response to life experiences, and of course the degree of confidence you feel changes according to circumstances. Think of the couple at the party. Let's add a few facts to help explain the difference in physical tension in each of our two subjects.

The man is an actor fresh out of drama school. He considers himself a fairly shy person with strangers though he knows he can be extrovert with his friends. He really only came to the party because an actor-friend said that some influential people might be there. He doesn't want to be thought of as lacking ambition, but right now he feels out of place and would much sooner slip off home.

The woman he is speaking with is a television casting director. Successful in her work, she prides herself on being friendly and approachable despite the power she exerts in her job. She is a skilled questioner and has decided to find out more about this man. She is confident, in control, and happy to be doing what she is doing. The man though is suffering a conflict: his animal instincts are telling him to retreat, but his mind is telling him he must stay and be sociable with this woman. Result: he is tense, she is relaxed.

Of course it's not quite even that straightforward. Though she's not aware of it, the woman has some unnecessary tension in her jaw and in her right foot.

She is finding conversation with the man hard work and has picked up on his unease. As she listens, she is also mentally scripting her polite exit from this situation.

Acting tips

Tension is the enemy of effective performance. It strangles vocal resonance and inhibits physical spontaneity. Before you can use tension effectively as an actor, you need to be able to relax at the drop of a hat. Painters need a blank canvas for their work; they create from there. A fully relaxed body is the actor's blank canvas; you create from that.

The actor in performance should use added tension with care. The voice is especially susceptible to damage from tension so try to avoid, even when playing a very tense character, centering your character's stress in the throat or neck. There are other ways to reveal and experience mental unease, for example, through slight tensing of more visible parts of the body such as your fingers and feet or through other means such as vocal changes (the note of the voice may be higher than usual, for example). Of course with practice and training you shouldn't need to be thinking about such things in performance, but while you're still developing control over your body signs, such awareness is valuable.

Recently I've started asking my acting students to conduct what I call a 'self-scan'. Typically, I ambush them when they're standing alongside their fellow students (we tend to work in circles), prompting them to share observations of their own physical and mental state on a moment-by-moment basis. Someone might say, for example, 'My mouth is tense because I'm smiling – I really enjoyed that last drama game', or, 'My right foot is tense because I was just reliving kicking the goal I scored yesterday'. I'm applying this self-scanning exercise to tension here, but you can of course scan yourself for all five of the THOSE behaviours.

An extension of this requires you to split your responses between actor and character during a rehearsal. You might say, 'As an actor, I'm tense in my face and neck, perhaps because I'm not sure I prepared well enough for this scene. As a character, my stomach is tense because I'm pulling it in to look slim' and so on. I realise this is potentially controversial – some will demand that you feel entirely in character whenever you're acting, even during rehearsal. However, my view is that a part of you must always be able to stand back and appraise things calmly so that you can take remedial action where necessary.

Exercises: Solo

1 Practise relaxing your body as fully as you can laying flat on the floor. Tense and then relax each set of muscles in your body, starting with the toes and working through to your face. Try to breathe normally as you tense and relax. You might find it useful to learn or record the words in the Appendix as mentioned earlier (Relaxation Exercise with Visualisation).

2 Practise relaxing your body as fully as you can while standing.

3 Select a specific point in your body. Tense that point and move around with that point still tensed. Make a mental note of how the tensing of that point affects you. Add one or two other points of tension and note how your brain starts to engage with your bodily stress. Your mind is looking to justify the stress in a rational way, perhaps by suggesting a reason for being uncomfortable.

4 Observe people's points of tension at any social gathering. Notice unnecessary tension in people's bodies, and ask yourself what might motivate their tension. Try imitating their tension. Be imaginative.

Exercises: Partnered

1 Using a scale of one to ten, you and your partner should each choose a level of confidence in social situations: ten is

high, one is low. Create a 'back story' to support your feelings. Enter a set situation when ready, maintaining an appropriate degree of tension. Stay aware of your tension in the scene, but behave as truthfully as you can.

2 Two people are talking. One (a tense person) wants to get away; the other (a relaxed person) is happy to stay talking. The tense person in fact seems relaxed, but subtly 'leaks' tension, e.g. nodding more than necessary, rubbing fingers together, smiling fixedly. Choose a location and two characters – and decide why the first one is tense and the other is relaxed. Again, stay aware of your tension in the scene, but behave as truthfully as you can.

Example: Natasha from *Three Sisters*

Read and rehearse the scene below from Act One, in which we first meet Natasha. Pay close attention to how the psychological pressure she experiences as a result of being on show, and at having made a wrong choice of what to wear, might show itself through hidden tension:

[Enter NATALIA IVANOVA; she wears a pink dress and a green sash.]

NATASHA

They're already there for lunch ... I'm late ... *[Carefully examines herself in a mirror]* I think my hair's alright. ... *[Sees IRINA]* Dear Irina, best wishes! *[Kisses her firmly]* You've so many visitors – I feel quite ashamed ... How do you do, Baron!

OLGA *[Enters from dining-room]*

Here's Natalia. How are you, dear?

[They kiss.]

NATASHA

I was just saying 'Best Wishes' to Irina. I feel quite embarrassed, you've so many people here.

OLGA

Really, it's just family and friends. *[in a low voice, shocked]*
You're wearing a green sash! My dear, you shouldn't!

NATASHA

Does it mean something bad?

OLGA

No, it just doesn't work – it looks odd.

NATASHA *[unhappily]*

Really? But it's not really green, it's more dull than that ...

[Goes into dining-room with OLGA.]

Tool No. 5: Adjusting Height

We all achieve a natural height in adulthood. This is of course
something we can't really control, being set as it is by things such
as genes and nutrition. But whatever height you happen to be,
you alter it on a moment-by-moment basis. Often the changes in
height are subtle, but they can be big and decisive. At times your
decision to change height will be driven by a need for comfort,
such as straightening your spine when sat at a keyboard for a
long time. But you will also often raise or lower your body
beyond what is strictly necessary. Why?

People alter their height in order to claim a particular position
on the status seesaw. Picture the following stereotypical scene in
a 'posh' restaurant:

A young man, a first-time diner in this sort of establish-
ment, has brought his girlfriend here, partly to impress her.
He wants to seem confident and in control, but he now
feels out of his depth: he's not sure of the rules of etiquette
and he fears looking foolish. He's being attended to by a

waiter who privately disapproves of the young man and his 'type'. At first glance, the waiter could tell that the diner is in unfamiliar surroundings – he is slightly hunched as if he doesn't want to be noticed. The waiter likes to reflect the status and reputation of the restaurant so he holds himself in a raised but relaxed posture, with his head tipped back very slightly. When he first speaks to the young diner, the waiter's posture leaves the diner with the distinct impression that the waiter is talking down his nose at him despite the apparently friendly tone of the waiter's voice.

In the animal world, changes in height take place for solid practical reasons which have everything to do with survival. The hunter finds a position of height from which to seek prey (think of an eagle wheeling high above oblivious creatures on the ground). The hunted also use increased height at times to scour the horizon for threats (think of a meerkat at full stretch). Both hunter and hunted also lower their height for practical reasons. Picture a cat stalking a bird – the cat's whole body is kept low in order to be unseen. Picture, too, the reaction of a squirrel when it hears something threatening – it drops in height and freezes.

Humanimals – people – tend to alter their height in company. This often occurs when a person's job requires them to think about how they influence others. A police detective may remain standing when aggressively interrogating a suspect who is seated in order to press for a confession. A counsellor working with a child may sit on the floor to seem less threatening and so to encourage the child to speak.

People also alter their height in relation to others in social situations. A high-status player, when in the company of someone who is seated normally on a sofa, may sit on the arm – they prefer to look down on others. A low-status player will tend to reduce their relative height – they prefer to look up to others. Within a group of friends, there will usually be someone who prefers the floor or a beanbag to a place on the sofa.

Sometimes people claim height (and so higher status) as a way to mask their own lack of confidence – they feel more in control, if they are higher up than the other person. Think back to the restaurant scene. This time the waiter's intention is to make the young man feel relaxed and welcome. Meanwhile, the young man wants to be more convincingly at ease. The waiter retains his formal body height, which he feels is respectful to the diner – he is after all on duty. He does not though tilt his head upward, but keeps it level and relaxed. The young man avoids slouching and instead holds a more upright posture. But in truth he is sitting a little too upright to seem relaxed and comfortable.

My local pizza restaurant experimented recently with the height issue in relation to customers. Waiting staff would make a point of sitting down at the table with you to take your order. It was an interesting tactic – for me it felt more informal, more friendly, a discussion rather than a formal interaction. It did though require the waiter to enter your personal space – your table – not something people are used to in restaurants. And not all waiting staff managed the 'friendly' bit well. After about a month the policy was quietly dropped.

Acting tips

As with tension, height in performance is something which needs to be handled sensibly. If you stretch yourself too high or if you compress yourself too much, you will be adding tension which may harm your performance, especially your voice.

The extremes of use of height in performance are probably best reserved for broad comedy or for heightened drama such as the plays of the Restoration period. In everyday life we tend to be pretty subtle when changing height.

It's often valuable to see what happens if you try doing the opposite. Let's say that in rehearsal you're perched on the arm of a sofa in a scene with another actor who is standing. Your char-acters are arguing. You feel the need to rise and face the other actor, which would mean standing to match their height. Try instead sliding down from the arm onto the seat of the sofa. The resulting change in mood, driven perhaps by your character's desire to seem unthreatened, may form a more interesting and truthful choice.

Exercises: Solo

1 When out shopping, move around with your height raised above what is normal for you. Make a mental note of how the change affects you. Note how your brain starts to engage with the change. Your mind is looking to justify it – perhaps you start to feel more powerful, even a bit pompous. Try doing the opposite. Note whether other people's reactions to you change at all.

2 Observe people's use of height at a social gathering. Notice unnecessary changes in height, and ask yourself what might motivate them. Imitate them.

3 Select a short audition monologue you know well – one in which you are talking directly to someone else. Restage it, subtly altering your height at points where it seems psychologically appropriate. At times, you may change height because you feel in control. At other times, you change height because you're less confident. Changes in height should be fluid, subtle and responsive. Ask an observer to watch your revised performance. Chances are, the invisible onstage character you are addressing will become more visible to your observer.

Exercises: Partnered

1 Think of a formal work situation where people will often consciously alter their height when meeting and talking. Rehearse and then perform a short scene which shows this. Find out how it feels if the heights are reversed.

2 Think of a social situation where, because of their confidence levels, people may alter their height when meeting and talking. Rehearse and then perform a short scene which shows this. Find out how it feels if the heights are reversed.

Example: Natasha from *Three Sisters*

Read and rehearse the section of a scene below from Act One, which follows moments after the previous scene (when we first met Natasha). Pay close attention to how the psychological pressure Natasha experiences as a result of feeling ridiculed might show itself through changed height:

> *[Loud laughter; NATASHA runs out into the sitting-room, followed by ANDREI]*

ANDREI

Just ignore them! Wait ... do stop, please. ...

NATASHA

I feel ashamed ... I don't know what's the matter with me but they're all laughing at me. I know it wasn't nice of me to leave the table like that, but I can't cope ... I can't. *[Covers her face with her hands.]*

ANDREI

My dear, I beg you. I implore you – don't get upset. I assure you they're only joking, really they're kind people. My dear, sweet –, they're all kind and sincere people, and they love both you and me. Come over here to the window, they can't see us here ... *[Looks round.]*

NATASHA

I'm just not used to meeting people!

ANDREI

Oh, you're young – you're splendidly, beautifully young! My darling, don't be upset! Believe me, believe me ... I'm so happy, my soul is full of love, of joy ... They can't see us! They can't! Why, why or when did I fall in love with you – Oh, I can't understand anything. My dear, my pure darling, be my wife! I love you, love you ... as I've never before ... *[They kiss.]*

Tool No. 6: Adjusting Openness

Openness describes how much you expose or conceal the front of the body. The opposite extremes would be as follows: **Fully open** would mean that your legs are apart, your head is raised slightly to expose your neck, your arms are away from your torso (for example with your hands on hips or, if you're seated, your hands may be joined behind your head with fingers interlocked). **Fully closed** would leave you with your legs entwined, your head tilted down, and your arms folded tightly across chest or stomach. The degree of openness is one of the most influential bodily signs. You can make a strong initial judgement of a person's state of mind by looking at their openness from some distance away.

Animals' degree of openness tends to reveal how vulnerable they feel to attack from hunters. The ultimate degree of concealment and self-protection – the favoured defence posture among many animals – is the foetal position. Others instinctively make themselves as small and low as possible using the ground as part of their protective shield: think of a mouse caught in the open.

Under intense physical threat, humanimals may do either, but significantly they can also show a defensive physical response as a result of psychological, not just physical, threat.

So a humanimal's degree of openness or concealment gives real clues to their mental state. The posture adopted tends to reflect a person's degree of confidence and their sense of status relative to others present. Let's start with the stereotypes. Picture a poolside scene: a super-confident and well-muscled lifeguard is chatting up (and being chatted up by) a shy bather who is wearing her new bikini for the first time. He'll probably have his hands on his hips; she'll probably have her arms folded in front of her. His legs will be apart in on duty mode; hers probably slightly crossed if standing, tightly entwined if she is sitting. He is exposing his body shape, suggesting that he is unconcerned about threat. She is partially hiding hers, projecting vulnerability, inviting him (to follow the cliché) to protect her.

Of course it's rarely as straightforward as that. Sophisticated as we humanimals are, we tend to be pretty well aware of the signals we're giving out so we throw in a few big distractions. Time for a bit of role-reversal. Back to our couple at the poolside: let's add a few new bits of information. He is a little unconfident about his physique (not uncommon these days among bodybuilders – the so-called Adonis syndrome). She knows she looks striking in her new bikini. He finds her perceived superconfidence a bit too much – he prefers to feel in control in this developing relationship. She wants to know if he has the personality to match the body; she is struggling to get conversation out of him and is quickly losing interest. He, lost for words, pretends he is being super-vigilant at the poolside in case of any accidents. Both wish they could say something funny to lighten the mood, but nothing appropriate is coming to mind.

How might this new information show itself in their relative body postures? He, on duty and on show, probably tries to maintain a degree of openness – legs apart, head up – but he folds his arms over his chest to shore up his confidence (and make his biceps look bigger). Surprised at her lack of progress, she has dropped her head slightly. Her legs are uncrossed and her hands are on her hips, but she is starting to feel exposed. Just after he has folded his arms she does the same, partially mirroring his posture (so-called 'postural echo'). This feels instinctively more comfortable and gives one of them the confidence to risk a joke.

Contradictory signs – such as arms folded but legs apart – are a common part of people's interpersonal armoury – it throws the other person off the scent from reading a person's true feelings. But we humanimals are cleverer still: we commonly use inanimate objects to justify the degree of our openness or concealment.

One final visit to the poolside. Things are not going well and she is about to make her exit – he is, too. Each has one or two items – he has his lifeguard's whistle and wears sunglasses; she has a small shoulder bag, sunglasses resting on her head, and a towel draped around her shoulders. Earlier in the meeting she had lightly towel-dried her hair, requiring her to raise her arms and expose her chest. Keen now for an exit she has pulled the towel protectively around her shoulders. She has also dropped her sunglasses down over her eyes. Using both hands he adjusts his sunglasses on his head, so giving him an opening-up gesture which subtly increases his sense of confidence. He also puts the whistle in his mouth, supposedly in reaction to a bit of splashing going on in the pool, but in truth to excuse himself from the effort of making further conversation. She fishes in her bag for some loose change and, finding it, looks purposely in the direction of the poolside bar. After a few moments, and with little more than a nod and a smile from each of them, he toots briefly on his whistle and moves towards the pool while she moves off to the bar.

Acting tips

Most types of openness or protective behaviour will cause no harm to your technical acting performance though a really closed posture is going to reduce both your vocal resonance and your available breath. It's worth getting really familiar with this aspect of body language. It's one of the most instinctive so, when used sensitively in a scene with another actor, it can really help a scene to seem real. It's common for two people to shift postural openness in direct response to one another and such shifting tends to be very fluid. If you're tense onstage or on set, you run the risk of being left behind when your fellow actor shifts their degree of openness or concealment. A shift in openness can also offer an audience vital clues to your character's attitude towards a new arrival in the scene.

Exercises: Solo

1 Next time you find yourself under pressure in a public situation – at a party, for example – take note of your bodily openness. If you find you have closed up in some way, try adopting a clear open posture, e.g. hands on hips. Maintain

this for some time and see how it affects your own feelings. Note also whether other people alter their behaviour towards you.

2 Choose a modern naturalistic monologue you are comfortable with, which you know well, and which is delivered to an unseen onstage character. Restage it using your full knowledge of openness. You might make subtle use one or two appropriate small props in your self-redirection.

Exercises: Partnered

1 Openness in humanimals gives clues to the character's mental state. The amount of openness can reveal a person's confidence and their sense of relative status. There may be hidden thoughts or feelings which leak out. Think of a situation in which two people might meet. Using a scale of one to ten, choose a level of confidence for each of you: one is low, ten is high. Create a back story to support your behaviour. Enter the set situation when you're ready and behave as truthfully as you can. Stay aware of your openness during the scene.

2 A person may use openness to manipulate the reactions of others, e.g. pretending to be vulnerable in order to be chatted up at a party by a 'hunter'; pretending to be tough in a dangerous neighbourhood. Think of a situation in which this sort of need might arise when two people meet. Using a scale of one to ten, choose a level of confidence. Create a back story to support your behaviour. Before the scene begins, take on the character's normal 'real' openness. Then adopt the 'pretend' openness which is designed to manipulate the feelings and behaviour of the other person. Enter the set situation when you're ready. Concentrate on staying aware of the mental conflict in maintaining the 'pretend' openness during the scene.

3 People often make subtle use of objects when interacting with others. These can help boost confidence or can hide real feelings. Select some small items for possible use, e.g.

bag, newspaper, cell/mobile phone, mirror, glasses. Prepare as before, but use the items subtly during the scene to help you become more open or more concealed.

4 The degree of openness a person shows will be fluid and changing, depending on who they are with and how they are feeling. Openness reveals their sense of relative status. Think of a social situation in which two people meet. Plan a moment in your scene when something big changes the relative status between the two characters – e.g. a decision, or a revelation. Explore during the scene how openness alters in each character before, during and after the 'moment'. Try running the scene as (a) strangers, (b) friends, (c) lovers.

Example: Natasha from *Three Sisters*

Read and rehearse the scene below from the start of Act Two. Natasha, bearing a message, comes across husband Andrei. Consider how she might use her talk of the cold (she seems to have banned fires in the house) as an excuse for maintaining the security blanket of a closed posture. Perhaps when she mentions the entertainers she might open up a little as her sense of having some control returns – and, again, as she plots to have Irina moved out of her room:

> [Scene as before. It is 8 pm. A concertina can be heard outside in the street. No fire is lit. NATASHA enters wearing a housecoat and carrying a candle; she stops by the door which leads into ANDREI'S room.]

NATASHA

Andrei, what are you doing? Are you reading? It's nothing, I just ...

> [She opens another door, and looks in, then closes it]

No candle burning ...

ANDREI *[Enters with book in hand]*
What are you doing, Natasha?

NATASHA

I was just making sure there are no candles lit. It's Shrovetide, and that servant is overexcited – I'm making sure nothing bad happens. When I came through the dining room at midnight last night there was a candle burning. She wouldn't tell me who lit it. *[Puts down her candle]* What's the time?

ANDREI. *[Looks at his watch]*
Quarter past eight.

NATASHA

And Olga and Irina are not back yet. The poor things are still at work. Olga at her staff meeting, Irina at the telegraph office ... *[Sighs]* I said to your sister this morning, "Irina, darling, you must take care of yourself." But she just ignores me. Did you say quarter past eight? I'm worred little Bobik might be ill. Why is he so cold? He had a hot fever yesterday, but today he is quite cold ... I'm so worried!

ANDREI

It's all right, Natasha. The boy is fine.

NATASHA

We should change his diet. I'm so afraid. And the entertainers were due here after nine; they'd better not come, Andrei.

ANDREI

I don't know. After all, they were invited.

NATASHA

This morning, when our little boy woke up and saw me he

suddenly smiled. He knew it was me. 'Good morning, Bobik!' I said, 'good morning, darling.' And he laughed. Children understand, they understand very well. So I'll tell them not to let the entertainers in.

ANDREI *[Hesitatingly]*
Well really it's up to my sisters. This is their home.

NATASHA
This is their home too. I'll tell them – they're so kind. ... *[Going]* I ordered sour milk for supper. The doctor says you must eat sour milk and nothing else, or you'll never lose weight. *[Stops]* Bobik is so cold. I'm worried his room is too cold for him. We should put him in another room till the warm weather comes. Irina's room, for instance, is just right for a child: it's dry and it gets the sun all day. I'll tell her, she can share Olga's room for now. It's not as if she's at home in the daytime, she only sleeps here ... *[A pause]* Andrei, darling, why are you so silent?

ANDREI
I was just thinking ... There's really nothing to say ...

NATASHA
Yes ... there was something I wanted to tell you ... Oh, yes. Ferapont has come from the Council, he wants to see you.

ANDREI *[Yawns]*
Okay, send him in.

[NATASHA goes out]

Tool No. 7: Working on Eye Contact

The eyes, it's been said, are a mirror to the soul, and the eyes have it when it comes to communication between people. We use them to interpret other people, and to signal (or disguise) our own feelings and intentions.

What matters most is the direction and the duration of eye contact between people. The extreme opposites would of course be continuous eye contact and no eye contact. Also of interest is flickered eye contact when people look up briefly but choose not to hold eye contact.

In the animal world, full eye contact from a hunter indicates high status: 'You look tasty', the animal might be thinking. But high status can also be claimed as a result of giving no eye contact, which might be interpreted as 'you're not worth my attention'. Full eye contact from a creature which is hunted can also indicate readiness to flee: 'Are they still there?'. No eye contact from a hunted creature can also mean submission: 'I know you're the boss'. Flickered eye contact – looking up briefly, but always looking away first – can indicate an acceptance of a lower status: 'Hello, but I'm really no threat to you'.

With humanimals, it's often much the same. The main difference is, once again, that we routinely manipulate our behaviour for some hidden reason.

One stereotypical scenario that deals with eye contact might be the old-fashioned headmaster in school assembly, steering laser-beam eyes around the school hall in an attempt to spy potential trouble-makers. Under his fierce stare the pupils remain stock-still and resolutely avoid his eye.

It's important to keep in mind the simple idea of hunter/hunted roles in the animal kingdom as, so often, they find a parallel in human relationships. We humans still hunt and are hunted; it's just that we no longer eat each other. Instead, the typical modern humanimal hunts for status and for positions in relationships that provide a sense of power or security. And we do this in a range of subtle, sophisticated and, at times, seemingly contradictory ways.

We are, from an early age, aware of the use and effects of eye contact. But as we get older we become more sophisticated. A group of four-year-olds would show active disinterest in the company of a boring teacher: looking away, yawning, staring out of the window. Bored secondary school pupils might feign interest with occasional strong eye contact. University students trapped in a dull lecture might apply themselves with apparent fervour to the task of note-taking.

Eye contact between people shows interest or respect (or a lack of it). Full eye contact can mean either a high-status sense of your being in control or a low-status sense of you being controlled: blinking reduces your sense of power and control. Looking away first can show acceptance of lower status than the person who is looking at you or it can imply that you're losing interest in the person. If you want to be confident that you have 'read' the meaning behind a person's eye contact – especially if you're observing one of these 'either/or' situations – look for the tension in the face and the body. A person who is most at ease with high-status behaviour will make strong choices with their eye contact and will underpin this with a relaxed face and body.

Some interesting recent research explores how eye movement relates to mental recall such as remembering past events. Broadly speaking, if you're seeing images in your mind, your eyes look upwards as if you are looking at the images on a raised screen in front of you. If you're recalling or hearing sounds, your eyes tend to move to the side; if you're recalling or experiencing strong feelings, your eyes tend to move downwards. I think it's interesting for actors to explore this. Try to catch yourself when you are remembering things, and explore how the theory works with spontaneous experience too. I've noticed that when I'm listening to someone on the phone, my eyes tend to move subtly but quickly from side to side. I think this sort of awareness of the subtleties of behaviour is worth exploring. Once you've developed an ease and familiarity with such knowledge, it should make you a more resourceful, versatile and truthful actor. Just make sure that the tail doesn't wag the dog – in other words, use such ideas to support your work in rehearsal, but don't let them dictate.

Acting tips

How long would your character hold eye contact with another character? Don't worry about such detail. There are too many variables to make a technically correct answer in any circumstances. Just learn the basic theory, explore it in rehearsal, and trust your instincts in performance.

Keep this in mind though. Generally speaking, the better you know someone, the less you feel the need to give them regular eye contact. There's less need for you to supply them with visual signs, such as smiling and nodding, since you understand each other well and are unlikely to offend one another. Also, you will find yourself needing to look elsewhere in order to unearth the more personal thoughts and feelings that friends discuss. It's difficult to form complicated thoughts, or indeed to recall events, if you're looking straight into someone's eyes.

Exercises: Solo

1 Try altering your preferred personal use of eye contact for a day. If you tend to look away first, hold strong eye contact instead. Maintain this behaviour for some time and see how it affects your own feelings. Note also whether other people alter their behaviour towards you.

2 Choose a modern naturalistic monologue you're comfortable with and know well (select one in which there is another character in the scene even though your audience cannot see them). Restage the monologue, using your full knowledge of the subtleties of eye contact.

Exercises: Partnered

1 Think of a work-related situation in which a professional person may consciously alter their eye contact in relation to a customer or client. You can use previous examples if you

wish, e.g. detective/suspect, counsellor/child. Devise a short scene which shows this.

2 Think of a social situation in which two people, recent acquaintances, meet, but one of them wants to hide their real feelings. Devise the scene so that eye-contact is manipulated by that person to throw the other 'off the scent'.

3 Think of a situation in which two close friends are seated facing outwards on a bench. Devise the scene so that the friends' minimal level of eye contact reflects their level of familiarity. Run the scene again with almost constant eye contact. Discuss the difference in the 'feel' of the relationship.

4 Practise chatting with your partner with notably differing degrees of eye contact. Discuss afterwards how it was that different levels of eye contact affected your sense of what your partner was feeling towards you.

Example: Natasha from *Three Sisters*

Read and rehearse this longer scene below from Act Two. For the first time, we see Natasha in the company of most of the men including VERSHININ, BARON TUZENBACH, SOLENI, FEDOTIK (all army officers) and CHEBUTIKIN (an army doctor). MASHA and IRINA are also present, along with ANFISA (a servant).

This is a highly charged scene for Natasha – these important people are guests in her house. Her husband is absent from the room. If she is to compete with Masha and Irina for the attention of the men, she may be tempted to call on her personal power as claimed through her beauty. Consider how she might use her eyes to do this. Soleni's snub will doubtless affect her confidence with eye contact though she may want to hide this. Though she speaks little in the scene, her use of French to put down Masha at the end suggests she is still working hard to impress:

[A samovar (a type of large table kettle) is brought in; ANFISA attends to it; a little later NATASHA enters and helps by the table; SOLENI arrives and, after greetings, sits by the table.]

VERSHININ

What a wind!

MASHA

Yes, I've had enough of winter. I can't even remember what summer's like.

IRINA *[turning over cards]*

It's coming out, I see. We're moving to Moscow.

FEDOTIK

No, it's not coming out. Look, the eight was on the two of spades. *[Laughs]* So you're not going to Moscow.

CHEBUTIKIN *[Reading paper]*

Tsitsigar. Smallpox is raging here.

ANFISA *[Coming up to MASHA]*

Masha, have some tea, dear. *[To VERSHININ]* Here you are Colonel ... I'm sorry, I've forgotten your name ...

MASHA

Bring some here, Nanny. I'm not going over there.

IRINA

Nanny!

ANFISA

Coming, coming!

NATASHA *[To SOLENI]*

Babies understand perfectly. I said 'Good morning, Bobik;

good morning, dear!' And he looked at me in quite an special way. You think that's just a mother speaking; not at all. He's a wonderful child.

SOLENI

If he was my baby I'd roast him on a frying-pan and eat him.
[Takes his tumbler into the drawing-room and sits in a corner.]

NATASHA *[Covers her face in her hands]*

Vulgar, common man!

MASHA

I envy anyone who can't tell whether it's summer or winter. I think that if I were living in Moscow, I just wouldn't care about the weather.

VERSHININ

The other day I was reading the prison diary of a French cabinet minister. He'd been convicted for his part in the Panama scandal. With what joy, with what delight, he writes of the birds he could see through his cell window, birds he'd never noticed when he was a minister. Of course, now he's free again he notices birds no more than he did before. If you move to Moscow, soon you won't notice it either. There can be no happiness for us, it only exists in our longing for it.

TUZENBACH. *[Takes cardboard box from the table]*

Where are the pastries?

IRINA

Soleni's eaten them.

TUZENBACH

All of them?

ANFISA *[Serving tea]*

There's a letter for you.

VERSHININ

For me? *[Takes the letter]* From my daughter. *[Reads]* Yes, of course ... *[to MASHA]* I have to go. I'm sorry, I shan't have tea after all. *[Stands up, agitated]* The same old story ...

MASHA

What is it? Is it a secret?

VERSHININ *[Quietly]*

My wife has taken poison again. I have to go. I'll leave quietly. It's all so unpleasant. *[Kisses MASHA'S hand]* My dear, my splendid, good woman ... I'll slip out this way. *[Exit.]*

ANFISA

Where's he gone? I've just poured his tea ... What a man.

MASHA *[Angrily]*

Be quiet! Fussing about so much I don't get a moment's peace! ... *[Goes to the table with her cup]* I'm sick of you, old woman!

ANFISA

My dear! Why are you like this?

ANDREI'S VOICE

Anfisa!

ANFISA *[Mimicking him]*

'Anfisa!' He just sits there and ... *[Exit.]*

MASHA *[In the dining-room, by the table, angrily]*

Let me sit down! *[Disturbs the cards on the table]* Look at you, spreading out your cards and taking up all the space. Drink your tea!

IRINA
You're in a mood, Masha.

MASHA
Well if I'm in a mood don't talk to me. Don't touch me!

CHEBUTIKIN *[laughing]*
Don't touch her, don't touch her ...

MASHA
You're sixty, but you're like a six-year-old, always up to some horrible mischief.

NATASHA *[Sighs]*
Dear Masha, do you have to act like this in public? With your wonderful looks you could be so enchanting in good society – if it wasn't – to be frank – for the things you say. – Je vous prie pardonnez moi, Marie, mais vous avez des manières un peu grossières ...

TUZENBACH *[trying not to laugh]*
Could I – could I have ... I think there's some cognac ...

NATASHA
– Il parait, que mon Bobik déjà ne dort pas, – he's woken up. He's not very well to-day. I must go and check on him, excuse me ... *[Exit.]*

Tool No. 8: Adjusting Space

Space is really the odd one out – the Joker. It's not, after all, something you actually do with your own body – it's something around you which you use or decide not to use. What's important is to understand how you move within space when other people are nearby – how much or how little physical space you claim compared to your immediate neighbour. This is your personal space. Imagine it as a flexible invisible bubble. People sense when they have pressed up against your bubble and you know when you've encroached on someone else's. People claim space through their bodily size and movement, and through their attitude. So to understand space in relation to bodies you need to be familiar with the other four characteristics of movement – **tension**, **height**, **openness**, and **eye contact**. All four variables allow you to claim or abandon the space that another person might want.

In the animal world, things tend to be pretty straightforward. (I like the old joke. Q. Where does a crocodile sleep? A. Exactly where it likes.) The degree of relative threat normally determines claims on space: lions lounge in the open, spread over a large area; sheep at night tend to huddle together.

Of course humanimals have to make things more complicated. Use of space is more often a reflection of a person's sense of status relative to others. As a result, we engage in daily tussles for space at the breakfast table, on the road to work, in the office, in bed. It is possible to claim a large space – and so a high status – through formal or informal use of objects. Picture the caricature of a pompous managing director with a huge desk covering most of their office while their lowly PA is perched behind a tiny desk outside the office door. Or picture two strangers facing each other on a train, a small shared table between them. The large-space-claimer uses bodily openness, height, a relaxed posture, and confident eye contact to stake their claim. This is backed up with assertive use of props – a bag takes up the seat beside them, a can of drink is placed at a point more than halfway across the small shared table, and when they occasionally cough they do so with head up. The small-space-claimer uses small and restricted body movement; their bag stays on their knee and their drink stays firmly on their side of the table. When they cough they do so into their own small space, turning head down and towards the window. These two characters are basically happy with their respective claims on space. Where things get more interesting is when two people disagree on allocation of space or when circumstances demand that the rules be suspended.

The first time I ask a new group of students to form a circle, I'm always left with enough space either side of me for at least one, possibly two, people. This is the space allocated to me out of respect, shyness, or simply wariness. By week two the space between each of us is the same.

Famous people are often allocated a large space whether they like it or not. A friend described finding a world-famous composer marooned alone in the middle of a room at a party, complaining distressfully that 'no-one is talking to me!'. Years ago at an awards ceremony in London, I was getting ready in my shared dressing room when we were visited by Queen front man Freddie Mercury. He had two 'minders' with him, but there may as well have been ten: the space we allocated to this shy icon seemed to push the rest of us right up against the walls.

Next time you're in a lift with other people, take a moment to observe the way people claim space around them. Interesting things happen in lifts where available space is small and unalterable. You don't know, as you wait for the lift doors to open, who will already be in there or how many people there will be. You don't know those people's sense of status which will determine their claim on the limited space available. You don't know whether the people already in there are strangers or acquaintances. When the doors open, you have to react instantly, claiming space according to who is already there. Most people therefore claim a small space, at least to begin with. People who claim a large space can quickly seem quite rude as they invade the unspoken neutral space allocated by others in the lift. In a crowded lift you would need the hide of a rhinoceros to demand a very large space.

People react unconsciously to other people's invisible bubbles, almost as if they feel the pressing skin of the other person's space. The head and body of the lower-status person will usually be turned slightly away from the power-holder. Thus people's sense of awareness of the size of another person's space – their bubble – can often be partly read through the direction they choose to face. When there's no available space – on an over-crowded underground train, for example – passengers sardined together into a carriage tend still to face in different directions so that the challenge of eye contact is kept to a minimum.

It's all very different though with friends. They are generally perfectly happy to share space. Sometimes people who are not friends remain insensitive to other people's spacial needs; such space invaders can cause much discomfort to others. This can be due to personality, but also to culture. Once, in Spain, I was mistaken for a local by an English couple seated in a bar. Though I sat a good six feet away from them, I overheard the woman mutter darkly (in English) that they were being 'encroached upon'. People from certain cultures can, it seems, prefer a much larger buffer zone than others.

Acting tips

An awareness of issues to do with the use of space between people is invaluable for an actor who wants to replicate natura-listic human behaviour. This is one area in which you should dare to trust your instincts moment-by-moment. Indeed, unless lighting or camera angles dicate otherwise, the use of space between you and your fellow actors ought to at least subtly change from performance to performance. Movement within space is something we do in reaction as well as when taking action. So if you really are psychologically tuned in to your fellow actors, there will be a fluid and changing use of space in response to your interaction with them. Once again muscular tension brought on by a mental state of unreadiness is the most inhibiting factor in relation to the effective use of space onstage. You have to be able to feel in character and focus hard on the

other onstage characters before your reactions can be spontaneous and authentic. Get rid of your script as early as possible in
rehearsal. Practise listening.

One interesting rehearsal technique requires the actors in a
scene to make moment-by-moment choices about use of the
space between their characters. Briefly, you run a scene and at
any moment you have to do one of three things: keep still, move
closer to another character, or move away from another character. At the rehearsal stage this activity is intended to promote
discovery, to allow each character to externalise feelings experienced towards other characters, so movement should be decisive
and significant. As rehearsals progress such movement may
become more subtle or may even disappear. A character may be
left with a yearning to move away from another character, but is
inhibited by some important factor such as pride, or the wish to
hide real feelings. What remains then is a hidden and appropriate
sense of tension – as it were, a body full of atoms wanting to go
there, but having to stay *here*.

Another way of visualising this as a psychological tension is to
imagine that your character is anchored somewhere – perhaps
even somewhere offstage – at a location that is a constant pull for
you. Then imagine a giant, strong elastic band that keeps trying
to pull you back to the anchoring point: the further away from it
you go, the stronger the pull back to the anchoring point. This
can work very well in a conflict scene when characters secretly
know things are going too far.

Exercises: Solo

1 Next time you find yourself in a confined space with others
  – on a train, for example, or in a lift – try to visualise the
  proportions of your personal space bubble. Then visualise
  it as being much bigger. Allow yourself some bodily movement which expresses the sense that you have a much larger
  personal space. Maintain this for some time and see how it
  affects your own feelings. Note also whether other people
  alter their behaviour towards you.

2 Choose a modern naturalistic monologue you're comfortable with and know well. Select one in which there is another character in the scene, even though your audience cannot see them. Restage the monologue using your full knowledge of space issues in relation to other people. Remember to be aware of the other character moving in space, too.

Exercises: Partnered

1 Think of a situation in which two strangers might meet. Using a scale of one to ten, choose a level of confidence for each of you: low, medium, or high. Create a back story to support your behaviour. Enter the set situation when you're ready, and behave as truthfully as you can within the situation. As an actor, concentrate on staying aware of your use of space during the scene. Run the scene again – but this time the characters are friends.

2 People sometimes use objects to help them claim space in relation to others. Select some small items for possible use – the ones you used in the Openness exercises will do. Prepare a scene which requires that there should be a table between characters. During the scene, make strategic use of your items to help you either to claim more space or withdraw into a smaller space.

3 Think of a social situation in which two people might meet. Plan a moment in your scene when something big changes the relative status between the two characters – a decision perhaps or a revelation. Explore during the scene how each character's claim on space alters before, during and after the moment. Try running the scene as (a) strangers, (b) friends, (c) lovers.

4 Run a scene in a lift in which both characters are comfortable with the relative space between them. Re-run the scene with one of the characters showing insensitivity towards the other character's spacial claim. If you have more than two actors, add additional characters to explore how new arrivals complicate things.

Example: Natasha from *Three Sisters*

Read and rehearse this scene below, again from Act Two. This is a tricky scene for Natasha. Guests are still in her house and, though her husband is here too, she seems to have made arrangements for her lover Protopopov to call and take her out. As she juggles these matters, and as she then confronts Irina with her decision to move her into Olga's room, her use of space could be valuable in suggesting her state of mind:

> *[NATASHA enters with a candle; she looks in through one door, then through another, and goes past the door leading to her husband's room.]*

NATASHA

Andrei's in there. Let him carry on reading. *[to SOLENI]* Sorry – I didn't know you were here – I didn't think we had visitors ...

SOLENI

It's all the same to me. Good-bye! *[Exit.]*

NATASHA *[To IRINA]*

You're so tired, my poor dear girl! [Kisses her] You should go to bed earlier.

IRINA

Is Bobik asleep?

NATASHA

Yes, but he's restless. By the way, dear, I wanted to tell you, but either you weren't at home, or I was busy ... Bobik's nursery is rather cold and damp. And your room would be so much better for the child. My dear, do move over to Olga's for a bit!

IRINA *[Not understanding]*
Move where?

[The bells of a troika are heard as it drives up to the house.]

NATASHA
You and Olga can share a room, for the time being, and Bobik can have yours. He's such a darling; I said to him today, 'Bobik, you're mine! Mine!' And he looked at me with those dear little eyes. *[A bell rings]* It must be Olga. She's so late! *[The maid enters and whispers to NATASHA]* Protopopov? What an odd man to do such a thing. Protopopov's come and wants me to go for a drive with him in his troika. *[Laughs]* How funny these men are ... *[A bell rings]* Somebody else is here. I could go for a quick half-hour drive ... *[To the maid]* Tell him I won't be long. *[Bell rings]* The doorbell – must be Olga.

[Exit.]

Example: *Polar Bears* by Mark Haddon
This scene, which is taken from close to the beginning of Haddon's play, provides two actors with an opportunity to explore initially contrasting THOSE behaviour that quickly starts to equalise as the scene develops and shocking news is revealed.

SANDY
John?

JOHN
Thanks. Thanks for coming.

SANDY
John, what's the matter?

JOHN

I don't really know where to start.

SANDY

Is this the disciplinary stuff at college?

JOHN

What? Oh, no, it's nothing to do with that.

SANDY

So, what is it then?

JOHN

I'm so sorry about this.

SANDY

Just tell me, OK.

JOHN

I shouldn't have called you.

SANDY

I'm family. You're meant to call me.

JOHN

I suspect you're not going to think of me as family after this. In fact, technically, I'm not sure I count as family any longer.

SANDY

Are you having an affair?

JOHN

No. I'm not having an affair. I've never had an affair. Never thought about having an affair. Which is pretty amazing, don't you think? In the circumstances.

SANDY

    Is Kay having an affair?

JOHN

    No, Kay's not having an affair. I'm pretty sure she wasn't. It's hard to be certain about that kind of thing.

SANDY

    Has something happened in Oslo?

JOHN

    Kay's not in Oslo.

SANDY

    No?

JOHN

    Have you got a cigarette?

SANDY

    Sure.

He gives John a cigarette.

JOHN

    Thanks.

SANDY

    So where is she?

JOHN

    She's in the cellar.

SANDY

    What's she doing in the cellar?

JOHN

She's dead.

SANDY

You said she was in the cellar.

JOHN

She's dead. And she's in the cellar.

SANDY

What are you talking about?

JOHN

Ironically, she didn't kill herself. If that's what you're thinking.

SANDY

Whoa, John. Don't fuck around like this.

JOHN

You see, actually, I killed her.

Pause.

We had a fight. Like we do, periodically. I pushed her and she fell. There was such a small amount of blood. You expect there to be a lot of blood, don't you? From seeing people being killed on the television.

SANDY

Oh, Christ.

section 4: **the voice**

Voice is quite simply the sound you make when the edges of your vocal cords vibrate. Speech builds on this sound: it is the use of (mainly) lips and tongue to manipulate that sound into words. In this Section we're concerned mainly with voice and how it supports the meaning of speech.

Actors use their skill with voice to ensure effective communication to an audience and to express things which may be hidden 'behind' the spoken words in a script.

We will now consider four new Tools which expand your range as an expressive performer.

Tool Number 9 – Adjusting Loudness – takes a common-sense look at one of the key elements of effective onstage performance.

Tool Number 10 – Adjusting Inflection – explores how changes in the musical notes in your voice can carry emotion, and can radically alter the meaning of words or phrases.

Tool Number 11 – Adjusting Note – examines how a character's 'true root note' can alter audience perceptions and develops the link between Note and Inflection.

Tool Number 12 – Adjusting Tone – assesses how the 'hardness' or 'softness' of a character's tone of voice can carry important associations.

As before, we'll look first at what each term means. We'll look behind the term to see what knowledge is required to be able to change each variable. We'll consider the psychological reasons why the relevant characteristic will vary from person to person, and I'll end with some suggested exercises to help you improve your control over each vocal characteristic.

Just as two people's physical behaviour can be very different, so too can there be huge variations in two people's vocal behaviour. Just as parts of your own body language may be wrong for a character you're playing, so too can aspects of your own vocal behaviour be inappropriate. It's important that you develop an understanding of the characteristics of your own voice and speech so that you can use that knowledge in practice as an actor.

What then are the key variables in voice? The word **LINT** captures the four key changeables: **L**oudness, **I**nflection, **N**ote, and **T**one.

Ideally you should use a digital recorder or similar to help you work through the vocal sections of this book. Record and replay your efforts as much as possible – you should get used to hearing even the subtlest differences in your own voice. With practice and a good ear – an ability to subtly differentiate between sounds – you will be amazed at how vocally versatile you can become. If you do manage to obtain a digital recorder, it's useful to be able to copy your recordings onto a computer – both for storing progress and, if you have the software, because there are adventures to be had in digitally messing with your voice.

Tool No. 9: Adjusting Loudness

Your own natural voice will be loud, quiet, or somewhere in between. What you have to do as an actor is to develop the control and sensitivity needed to vary volume. The basic reason is obvious: the audience member sitting high up in a theatre's gods must be able to hear all the words spoken by you every bit as clearly as the person sitting in the front row of the stalls.

In a moment we'll look at the techniques of volume control. First though let's put the issue of vocal volume into context in everyday life. Vocal volume in the real world can reveal important psychological things about a person. Let's start with the clichés: a confident person is always loud; a shy person is always quiet. Like most clichés, there's a lot of truth in this. Confidence – real, unforced confidence – may well be expressed in part through a loud, clear voice. The speaker is secure in their opinions and is happy for anyone to hear them. A shy person, meanwhile, lacks confidence in their ability to communicate well. They may doubt the appropriateness of their own opinion. In an effort to limit damage to their confidence, they tend to be vocally quiet.

So far, so obvious. But, as with physical communication, things get rather more interesting when the speaker tries to disguise their feelings. Someone who normally thinks of themselves as being shy, may find themselves in a situation where they must seem confident – making a speech at a wedding, for example. So they do their best to be vocally louder. If they're sufficiently in control, then they do a good job disguising their shyness and manage to sound confident. If the stress of the situation takes over, they may actually speak far too loudly. Consider also the super-confident person who is attracted to a shy person at a party. The former responds to the need to avoid bulldozing the latter by adopting a quieter, more intimate vocal level.

How then do you gain control over vocal volume? As with so many other things, you learn the theory, you explore the processes, and you practise, practise, practise.

Here in brief is the process which leads to you creating vocal sound:

- You take a breath.
- You breathe out.
- As you breathe out, some of the air passes over the vocal cords in your throat.

- You allow the air to vibrate the edges of the vocal cords.
- The sound you produce is your voice.

So far, so straightforward. So how do actors gain greater control over vocal volume?

Mainly, they learn to relax under pressure. A relaxed body is a body freed of muscular tension. It's no coincidence that vocal exercises are often done with the student laid flat on the floor: this position requires virtually no muscle tension.

There are real benefits to being able to stay physically relaxed during performance. You can take a bigger breath. You have greater control over the outward flow of breath. Resonance, which helps to amplify your voice, will be enhanced.

Resonance occurs when sound is amplified through effective use of resonators. Resonators are spaces: chambers of varying size, dotted about your upper body. Your mouth is a resonator and so is your nose, your throat, your sinuses and – to some extent – your lungs. Each of these resonators has the potential to help your voice to become amplified – to carry better across a space. Picture two guitars. One is a solid-bodied electric guitar, the other is a hollow-bodied acoustic guitar. If you strum the strings on the electric guitar without plugging it into an amplifier, you might struggle to hear the resulting sound from across a small room. If you do the same thing to the acoustic guitar, the sound resonates in the hollow body of the guitar, amplifying the sound hugely. The hollow body of the guitar is the guitar's resonator.

How can we be sure that it is the empty space which is responsible for amplifying the guitar's sound? If you fill the hollow body of the guitar with some sort of material – cotton-wool, say, or cloth – the reduction in the availability of empty space in the hollow body causes a massive reduction in resonance, which leads to a significant reduction in volume. It's the same with the human body. If you're very tense, you start to restrict and reduce your resonators so you get less amplification through resonance. If you have a bad cold and your nose and sinuses are blocked, you will notice a marked reduction in volume. This deadening effect results mainly from the blocked resonators being inactive.

There's already a great deal of help and advice available to support the actor who wants to improve vocal projection (see Further Reading), so, with apologies, I'm going to move on.

Acting tips

There's not too much benefit in analysing the psychology behind levels of vocal volume, for the simple reason that an actor onstage must clearly maintain a significant level of volume whatever their character's given circumstances. The need to be heard must override any notions of realism: this is a simple golden rule, a given. An audience may sometimes forgive less than brilliant acting. If you speak too quietly and you deny them access to the story, they'll not forgive that. Incidentally, this is also true in the recorded media. If the director can't hear all of your words, you'll be stopped and there will be a retake. The sound recordist will try to take account of your vocal volume, but you may be asked speak up or even reduce your vocal volume. This is harder than it sounds if you're working on an emotional scene. Always remember though that you're operating in a commercial environment, someone in the hierarchy has deemed that the words matter. Just do your best – it's unlikely that people will notice your private awkwardness.

Exercises: Solo

Here is a list of exercises to do in sequence, which will help you to achieve greater vocal volume. Make sure your body is in a relaxed position before you start each exercise.

1 Lie on the floor, face up, and relax your body fully. Breathe regularly through your nose imagining, as you breathe in, that your navel is being drawn towards the ceiling. (This helps to ensure that your breathing makes use of your diaphragm muscle, which is located just above your navel.) Let your teeth be parted but keep your lips together. As you

breathe out, allow the air to pass over your vocal cords so that you make the gentlest of sounds. Don't try to form any words, just make a simple sound: you are gently activating the vocal cords and amplifying the sound through your natural resonators. The sound you make, a gentle 'mmmm' sound, should be roughly on the same note, but, because you're not singing, the note will glide downwards a little as you run out of breath. You should feel a slight tickling sensation on your lips.

2 This is a continuation of the first exercise. This time, as you breathe out, after three seconds let your jaw drop so that your mouth falls open: visualise the sound as being released from confinement. The sound you make will be a gentle 'mmmaaah'. With some practice, you'll notice that, with relatively little effort from you and without any attempt to shout, your voice is surprisingly loud. Check for tension: your mouth and throat are large resonators which will work more effectively as resonators if they are open and relaxed. Yawn, noticing the open position of the throat and the back of your mouth. Aim for a relaxed version of this position when you're breathing out. Practise this exercise daily. You'll become familiar with the power of resonance and you will also get used to being relaxed when you create sound.

3 Do as you did before in 2, but also practise controlling the flow of breath more carefully. Count in your head how many seconds you take to breathe in then to breathe out. In normal speech, we tend to take a very short breath in and then we control the outward flow of air over a period of a few seconds. Be aware that when you work on verse or classical texts, you can't always take a breath when you feel like it – you may need to wait until the end of a long line. Over time, train yourself to be able to take a big breath, which you release in a controlled way through a relaxed body, making good use of your resonators.

4 Repeat the exercises above, but do them standing up. Stand with your feet slightly apart, your weight evenly balanced,

arms by your sides. You need few muscles to stay in this position – mainly just the muscles around your ankles and your knees. Keep everything else as relaxed as possible. The challenge is to maintain strong amplification through use of your resonators, even though some muscles need to be tensed. Note just how few muscle groups are required to stand like this. Later, when you're in a social situation, notice how many more muscles you use – frowning, tensing the jaw, pressing thumb against fingers, clawing feet, tilting neck at an angle, placing weight mainly on one hip – these are some of the common areas of added tension we noted earlier in the book. As an actor you need to develop an awareness of which muscles are tense, so that you can isolate and relax those which are tensed unnecessarily.

Tool No. 10: Adjusting Inflection

Inflection describes the way in which we move through different notes when we use our voices.

As you'll see, we do tend to think of inflection as a characteristic of speech rather than of voice. But I'm going to cheat and introduce it here in the section on Voice, not just because you can actually alter inflection without using language, but because we often do. And when we do, vocal inflection is often inextricably linked to our spontaneous emotions. A yawn, for example, requires you to make a simple non-speech sound, which typically slides from a higher note to a lower one. And a yawn can carry considerable meaning in terms of a person's attitude and state of mind. Try a few pretend yawns now and widen the range of notes which you pass through as you yawn. Think also of the 'mmm!' sound we make when something tastes good: without use of words, the voice slides from one note to another. The vocal sound which accompanies any intense sensual or psychological experience – pain, laughter, orgasm – each can easily be voiced using a non-speech-based change in inflection.

To consider how we alter inflection, it's probably easiest to think, initially, about singing: a song with only one note would be extremely dull to listen to, so the composer guides the singer through a variety of notes during the piece. Think of the old rhyming song 'Three Blind Mice'. It begins with three simple notes: a high note for 'three', a lower note for 'blind', and a lower note still for 'mice'. Fast-forward now to the section which runs, 'They all ran after the farmer's wife'. Sing it. (If you're reading this on a train, hum it. If you're reading this on a train, and you want more space around you, sing it.) This time, the melody uses four notes. The song follows a pattern which, during that particular line, uses most of those notes more than once. If the singer can read music, they may use a score, which will guide them in know- ing when a note is to be repeated. For a singer, a musical score is in essence a guide to inflection: it tells them whether the next note to be sung is higher, lower, or the same as the previous note.

In speech, vocal inflection helps the listener to follow meaning. At some point in your life you'll have come across the person who speaks in a monotonous voice (meaning they speak virtually on a single note). Have a go now at speaking on a single note. (This should get you even more space on the train.)

Not only would this be boring to listen to, it would be very difficult for the listener to pick out which parts of the spoken sentence are most important. So the speaker (even – if you listen carefully – the boring speaker) takes the trouble to vary the notes. There is another possibility – emphasising key words using increased vocal volume only on those words. (Try this on a train if you want the *whole carriage* to yourself.) Keep your voice inter- esting by varying the notes.

Now look at the last sentence ('Keep your voice interesting by varying the notes'). Imagine you're about to make a speech, and this sentence is the first line of your speech. Decide for yourself which are the most important words in the sentence (pick a maximum of four).

One interpretation would give the following capitalised words the most importance:

KEEP your voice INTERESTING by VARYING the NOTES

Read the sentence out loud, stressing the words which are in capitals.

In order to stress the words in capitals, you will need to vary the notes. Most likely, you will have used a slightly higher note for the words in capitals. As I said earlier, it's a good idea to have a recorder with you when you're doing exercises like this. If you have one, use it now, repeating the sentence and accentuating the words which need stressing. Play it back and listen for the (possibly subtle) changes in use of note.

Listening to a speaker is not, of course, the same as listening to a singer. A singer follows notes which a composer has previously scored. Even the length of time a note is held for will usually be predetermined. The speaker, however, is providing a spontaneous score and the resulting score reveals things about the speaker's feelings and attitudes.

There is another, fairly obvious, way in which the inflection of a speaker differs from the inflection of a singer. The singer has a fixed range of notes to choose from. If the singer fails to reach a note cleanly, the listener notices (and probably winces). The speaker has a range of notes in their repertoire determined by their vocal range. There's no such thing as being 'off key' for a speaker: pretty well anything goes so long as the chosen inflection supports the speaker's meaning.

Another difference: the speaker habitually slides between notes whereas the singer generally does not. Go back to the line from 'Three Blind Mice' which runs: 'They all ran after the farmer's wife'. Sing the line again. Now sing it a second time, but this time allow yourself to slide from one note to another (you'll probably sound drunk). Take it a little further. Start to think of the sentence as being a spoken sentence: you're telling the story to a child and the child asks: 'So what happened to the mice next?' You reply, 'They all ran after the farmer's wife'. When you say the line, keep in your mind the 'sung' version. Speak the line, keeping approximately to the notes in the 'sung' version, but try to make the sentence work as a genuine, spoken reply to the child's question. When you do this, you are consciously using vocal inflection.

Once you become aware of vocal inflection in speech, you can start to use it consciously. In my view actors do need to be conscious of, and able to control, inflection. Much of the time, actors' awareness of their use of inflection simply helps them to avoid sounding dull. But some jobs require an actor to be extremely competent in manipulating vocal inflection. Voice-over work for commercials relies on the actor being fully vocally responsive to the needs of the director. A director working with a voice-over artist will often ask the actor to alter emphasis on a particular word or phrase – this usually means they want a different vocal inflection.

Vocal inflection is something listeners respond to with great sensitivity. Out loud, say the phrase, 'That's interesting'. Sound as if you mean it, as if you've just read something that really impresses you. You'll probably find that you've spoken the line with a vocal inflection which rises significantly at some point during the phrase. Now say the phrase again, but this time artificially reduce the range of notes in your vocal inflection, limiting, as it were, the bandwidth. The statement will now sound less sincere, tinged (or laden) with irony or sarcasm. The words are the same; the vocal inflection, when altered, radically changes the message.

The use of a wide range of notes generally suggests enthusiasm and sincerity though too much variety in notes can tip you over into sounding insincere. Using a narrow range of notes, or under-inflecting, suggests a lack of enthusiasm or cynicism. Among some people, especially some teenagers, it is considered uncool to sound highly enthusiastic. The inflection pattern among such groups can be limited to a really narrow range of notes – partly, I imagine, in reaction to those authority figures who habitually (or through training) tend to use a wide and expressive vocal inflection. It's worth noting that if you under-inflect (i.e. reduce the bandwidth of notes you use) and combine this with an apparently interested facial expression, the mixed message can seem very sarcastic indeed.

Acting tips

Listen to vocal inflection around you and secretly mimic it. You're copying the pattern of notes, not the words, so you can get away with humming the inflections under your breath. Real conversations have a huge variety of inflection range. Most people are untrained in voice-use so they're fairly unaware of their inflection pattern. Regional accent is relevant here: some accents have very distinct vocal inflection patterns. Indeed with some accents you can often identify the accent just from the vocal inflection pattern without hearing any actual speech (the 'Brummy' or Birmingham accent in the United Kingdom is a good example).

Mimic also broadcasters – newsreaders, radio presenters, journalists. Journalists who deliver reports from the field often have peculiar inflection patterns which seem at times to have random stresses, but are accepted as part of the field reporter's voice. The person who reads the Saturday football results on UK television famously uses vocal inflection which is predictable: you know whether it's a home win, a draw, or an away win halfway through the announcement. Try the following score in different ways:

Liverpool	1	Arsenal	1
Chelsea	2	Newcastle United	0
Manchester United	0	Everton	5
		(Well – you never know.)	

Radio presenters' vocal inflection tends to reflect their listeners. Those broadcasting to a general, older audience can be heard using a pretty wide range of notes: they're trying to sound energised, enthusiastic, interesting, knowledgeable. In contrast, a presenter targeting a teenage audience will usually apply very limited inflection in order to sound unimpressed, cynical, cool.

Programmes aimed at a pre-school-age audience are different again: voices span a dizzying range of notes as presenters strive to combine a sense of enthusiasm with very clear communication.

Newsreaders use a wider or narrower range of notes depending on the news story. Most news is delivered with quite a wide range of notes to help clarify meaning, but the death of a well-loved celebrity is always delivered with a limited inflection. Try reading a selection of pieces from a newspaper with this in mind.

Exercises: Solo

1 Refer back to the exercises in the Loudness section. This time, as you breathe out, vary your vocal inflection, letting your voice slide upwards and down again. Increase the frequency of variation and use a wider range of notes each time (but avoid going into a falsetto voice). You'll probably notice as you do this that different resonators come into play, depending on the note you reach. On a high note you can feel vibration in your nose and forehead; on a low note you can feel it in your throat and chest.

2 Similar to 1, but using your imagination as a stimulus. First, let yourself release a plain, monotonous sound. Now concentrate on the image and taste of your favourite food. Let yourself release a vocal sound again, but this time allow your feelings towards this tasty food alter the inflection. Try it with other imagined stimuli – unpleasant as well as pleasant images, intensely pleasurable memories as well as not so pleasurable ones.

3 Pick a nursery rhyme. Sing it. Sing it again and again, slowly converting the singing into speech by sliding between notes. You'll probably find that you need to reduce the pitch of the highest notes in order to stop the piece sounding too 'sung'. Try to convert it from a sung rhyme to a spoken phrase without sacrificing all of the original tune, and try to allow some sort of spoken meaning to come through: try to make the inflection pattern make sense.

Exercises: Partnered

1 Have a conversation with your partner, but without using any words and (mostly) keeping your lips together. Instead, have an idea in your head of what the words would be, but just use voice. Varying the inflection will help your partner to understand your meaning. Try to avoid adding mimed gestures that compensate for the absence of words.

2 Refer back to the beginning of the section on Inflection. Select a range of wordless vocal sounds people use to express spontaneous feelings and attitudes: yawning, laughter, responses to physical pain or pleasure, reactions to mental moods of happiness or sadness. Working with your partner, devise a short scene in which an interaction takes place using only sounds and actions. You're actually devising a scene here so allow enough time to develop this wordless scene properly.

Tool No. 11: Adjusting Note

Every individual has a note which I'm calling the **true root note** for their voice. By this I mean that you have a natural vocal note which you make when you're fully relaxed, for example when you vocalise a yawn in private. You've probably already demonstrated your own true root note (this was the spontaneous vocal sound you made while completely relaxed in the first solo exercise in the Loudness section).

People do of course have different root notes. Partly this is physiological. Men tend to have larger and less tightened vocal cords and larger resonators (spaces) so they tend to have a lower root note which amplifies well. Women tend to have shorter and tighter vocal cords, which create a higher root note, and the resonators that accompany and amplify that higher note tend to be smaller.

In adulthood, some people develop a voice which is rooted at a pitch which is different from their true root note. The reason for developing such a 'public' root note – a higher or lower root note which a person uses in public and which becomes, by habit, the core of their 'new' voice – is usually psychological. Over a period of years people can become socialised into behaving in ways other people expect them to behave. For girls and women a soft-toned voice delivered on a fairly high note can seem appealing to men by dint of it sounding unthreatening. The caricature example of this has to be Marilyn Monroe. A girl who has a fairly low true root note (something to be valued in theatre acting) may be teased for having a manly voice. A higher true root voice in a man is often considered inappropriate (sportsman David Beckham has been mocked for having a voice which uses a lot of higher notes).

It's hardly surprising then that girls and women can lose contact with their lower true root note and develop instead a higher public root note. Men can adopt a voice which is centred at a note lower than their true root note in order to sound manly (a cultural counter-reaction, which raises the root note, is possible too).

This loss of contact with your true root note can become a problem if you're an actor. Partly this is to do with vocal projection. In theatre, a voice which uses a lot of high notes gains only limited support from resonators: the voice doesn't carry so well. Also, a voice which has developed away from its owner's true root note is not going to be as in contact with that person's emotions. So it's worth reflecting on whether this has happened to you and, if it has, you might want to rediscover your true root note. This is not as hard as it sounds, but it will take time. You'll need to do voice exercises regularly, and you'll need to monitor your voice use in everyday conversation. The first two solo exercises in the Loudness section should be repeated daily. Monitor your progress using a digital recorder. Work also on the exercises in the Inflection section – these will help you to reach any specific vocal note.

We're going to look in more detail now at the way in which vocalised notes can be combined to alter the meaning of a spoken phrase. We've had a first look at this in the previous Section. We're now going to explore in more detail the relationship between Note and Inflection.

For this section, you'll need to be familiar with the 'do-re-me' musical scale popularised in *The Sound of Music*. This musical scale simply places notes in order to form an octave (the series of eight notes which musicians and singers use as part of musical notation). You don't need to be able to read music.

Make sure first that you're relaxed so that your starting note is close to your true root note. Try a sound: that's your 'do'. Now hum out loud the first three notes – do, re, me. Hum the three notes a few times. Now hum them in the order me, do, re. Practise it a couple of times so that you can be sure that you've hit the right notes. Now take the word 'hello'. Sing the word 'hello', keeping the tune in the order which you've just been practicing: me, do, re. (You'll probably sound like a medieval monk.) Now repeat the word, but alter it so that you are sliding between the three notes. Practise this, imagining that you're greeting somebody. You're now using your conscious awareness of how notes form an inflection pattern within speech.

Take it a little further now. Go through the octave again, starting at do, and stop when you get to te. Work out and remember the simple sequence: te, do, re. Once again, using the word 'hello', transform this into a realistic spoken greeting. Practise it.

Think now about the difference between the two ways in which you spoke the word 'hello'. Technically, in the second version you started on a higher note. Ask yourself how the change of note might alter the meaning behind the greeting.

Here's one interpretation. The first time you say hello, you're not surprised to see the person, but you suspect that they might have been up to something. Your objective is, 'I want to know what you've been up to'. The second time you say hello, you're greeting someone you haven't seen for a long time and you're pleased to see them. Your objective is, 'I want you to stay and chat'.

Let's try a simple third version. This time, keep entirely on the note 'do' throughout the word 'hello'. In other words, say the word on low monotone. How does this sound? What could the meaning be behind this delivery of the greeting? Perhaps the person you're speaking to is someone you've been hiding from because they irritate you and they've just found you. Your objective might be, 'I want you to go away'.

One more to try. Go back to the first time you said 'hello'. You used the three notes in the order me, do, re. Hum 'do' again. Now sing your way up the octave so that you reach the next 'do' up (an octave above the previous one). Find the three notes 'me, do, re' within this higher octave. Convert this again into a greeting using the word 'hello'. How has the meaning changed? One interpretation is that, although you are still suspicious of the person, you really didn't expect to see them. Your objective is still, 'I want to know what you've been up to', but now you might also be wondering, 'how on earth did they know I would be here?'

Acting tip

I'm not, by the way, advocating that you should deconstruct a script, naturalistic or otherwise, in this way. It's a tortuous process at the best of times and you'll be guaranteed to lose some spontaneity if everything is rigidly pre-planned. The point of the exercises is to help you to see that the choice of note, and the pattern of inflection, do greatly matter to an audience – a listener will pick up on the most acute of subtleties if the actor is aware of what they are doing. When you're playing the sort of character who is adept at controlling their face and body to hide their real feelings – a high-status public figure for example – then vocal note and inflection become crucial to effective communication, both to your audience and to your fellow actors.

Exercises: Solo

1 Start to experiment with (temporarily) changing your own root note. Listen to, and mimic, voices on radio and television. As you listen, try to identify a note that seems central to the voice. Do this with a male and a female voice, and note the difference.

2 Adopt a noticeably different root note when you're briefly with strangers – buying something in an unfamiliar shop for example.

3 Make a subtler change of root note when you're with friends. Try to spot if there's any difference in the way they treat you.

4 Select a monologue from a naturalistic play. Record a good sight-reading of the speech on your digital recorder using a slow pace. Listen to the recording, paying close attention to the choices of note and inflection. Replay the speech, and, as the recording plays, speak the speech out loud again – this time making very different choices of root note and inflection. Record the second, different version of the speech as closely as you can from memory. Listen to both. Ask yourself how different meanings were created by the two different versions of the speech.

Exercises: Partnered

1 Begin a conversation with your partner about an easy subject such as 'favourite places'. As you speak, try to become aware of the root note and inflection pattern you are using during the conversation. Try if you can to create an imaginary retrospective score of this in your head as you hear the root note and inflection that you have just employed. Allow each other to pause and repeat short phrases as a way of noting the inflection pattern and under-lying root note.

2 Repeat the exercise. This time, place one hand in front if you with your forefinger pointing away from you. Each time you speak, let your forefinger rise or fall in response to the pattern of your vocal inflection (if you're speaking on a monotone, your finger will of course be still). Ask your partner to speak very slowly and use your hand to retro-spectively score their inflection pattern in the air. The lower the root note, the lower your finger is in the air.

3 Repeat the first exercise again. Pause regularly to repeat phrases of several words, using precisely the same choice of

notes and inflection that you have just spontaneously used. If you or your partner create any non-verbal sounds, note these too, and try to repeat them.

4 Below is the script for a situation in which two people might meet. Start to learn the script, being careful to vary the root note and the inflection pattern each time you repeat the script. Perform the scene several times, each time altering your character's root note and inflection. Start to notice how different choices of root note and different inflection patterns connect to the psychology of the speaker. For example, what thoughts and attitude might be suggested if you employ a low root note and highly limited inflection?

A: Hello.

B: Hello.

A: Cold, isn't it?

B: It is.

A: Have we met before?

B: Have we? I don't know.

A: I think we have.

B: When?

A: I don't know.

B: No.

Tool No. 12: Adjusting Tone

Tone is a term which is used to describe the degree of hardness or softness in the quality of a person's voice. It's difficult to describe and to identify tonal quality, but it can have a very strong impact on the listener.

There are similarities between the tone of a voice and the tone settings on a high-fidelity audio system. Many audio systems have controls which allow you to increase or reduce the strength of the bass, and treble qualities in music. More sophisticated systems allow you to alter the tone of a piece of music in very subtle ways through the use of a graphic equaliser: the bass, treble and middle frequencies can be balanced to levels which suit each individual listener. When you turn up the frequency control on, say, the bass section of an audio system, you are in effect increasing the degree of bass resonance and not just turning up the bass volume. If you already have the music turned up loud on a really powerful system, you can find that the bass notes in a piece of music vibrate so strongly through the speakers that you can feel vibration in your own body.

It's important to remember that vocal tone, as with musical tone, is a quality which can be altered when sound is pitched and held on a single note. Any note you can sing comfortably can be altered to have a harder, or a softer, tone.

Let's stick with the idea of vocal tone being hard or soft. What are the judgements that we, as listeners, attach to voices with hard or soft tonal qualities? A soft-toned voice tends to lend a speaker the sense of being gentle, thoughtful, relaxed. Caricature examples might be a child counsellor, or a Classic FM radio presenter. A hard-toned voice can make a speaker seem energised, spontaneous, tense. Caricature examples might be a market trader or a presenter on a youth TV channel.

As a general rule, a regional accent which is associated with a city tends to have a harsher tone than one associated with a rural area. People use their breath, tension and resonance in slightly different ways. People from rural Ireland, for example, tend to release a fairly smooth and continuous flow of air when speaking, which is more conducive to allowing vocal resonance. Natives of Belfast, however, tend to interrupt the flow of air quite a lot, which adds physical tension to the throat and so reduces resonance. They do this by use of what is known as a glottal stop. When considering vocal tone, it's worth clarifying precisely what a glottal stop is.

A **glottal stop** occurs when the back of the throat is momentarily tensed during speech, halting the flow of air. Say out loud the word 'automatic' with a strong stereotypical London Cockney accent. It comes out as 'au'o'ma'ic' with at least three glottal stops within that single word. Do it again. This time trap your delivery of the word after the first bit so that you say only 'au'. Note the position of your throat: it's tensed and closed – no air can get through.

Think back now to the section on Loudness, where we looked at resonance. Resonators work best when air is allowed to flow freely and the muscles around the resonators are relaxed. Vocal tone and whether a person's voice sounds hard or soft in tone, depends most of all on these two factors: flow of air and bodily tension.

So what can you do to alter the tone of your own voice? It's not easy to alter tone in any significant way. Vocal tone is like regional accent in that it's something which you've developed throughout your life and so has become instinctive. If you want to vary tone, you'll need to gain full control over both the flow of air when you're breathing out and the degree to which you are physically relaxed. It helps also to develop a sense of placement of the voice, visualising your voice as being centred at a particular point along the route of the flow of air. If you're trying to achieve a soft vocal tone, it can be helpful to visualise the voice as being placed in the centre of your chest. Keep as many muscles as possible relaxed and focus on feeling the vibration in your chest resonator (think Classic FM presenter). If you're trying to achieve a hard vocal tone, visualise the voice as been placed in the throat or in the mouth (think youth TV presenter). Be careful in live theatre though. Placing the voice in the throat will inevitably create some degree of muscle tension there, and if you're struggling to project your voice, tension can lead to long-term damage. In recorded media such as TV and radio such tension is sustainable as long as you're not having to project your voice.

Acting tip

Your own natural vocal tone will be located somewhere between hard and soft. The more extreme your tone is, the greater the need to develop the sensitivity to change it. So listen carefully to the differing vocal tone of ordinary people. Listen also to voice-overs for television and radio commercials. The type of product being marketed will dictate the choice of vocal tone used. Sometimes the same actor can be heard using different tones within different commercials. If you find that you can master the ability to alter tone, you may well become that bit more employable as an actor.

Exercises: Solo

Perform the following solo exercises daily, using your digital recorder to monitor your progress.

1 Go back to the first exercise in the Loudness section. Begin by repeating the original exercise. Then, as you breath out, experiment with subtle variations of tension which will alter your vocal tone. Use visualisation to place your voice at points on a range between the centre of your chest and your lips. The visualisation is intended as a mental guide only. Technically, you will be subtly adding muscular tension to harden the tone and removing tension to soften the tone.

2 Repeat Exercise 1, but this time maintain a relaxed muscular state and change the note each time you breathe out. Observe how your vocal tone seems to harden each time you choose an increasingly higher note and seems to soften when you use lower notes. Remember that, the lower the note, the more you are using chest and neck resonance.

3 Transcribe voice-over tag lines from television and radio commercials. Practise speaking the words using varying degrees of hard and soft tone. Record your work and listen to the differences.

Exercises: Partnered

1 Find a scene containing some dialogue between two characters (you could initially use the short dialogue above, in Partnered Exercise 4 in the Note section). Allocate a particular tone to each character – a hard tone for one and a soft tone for the other. Try to make sure that both characters use roughly the same root note. Read it aloud. Swap tones between characters. Discuss with your partner whether different qualities of tone seem to suit different characters. Try another duologue.

2 As before, but this time allow your characters to use significantly different root notes – one high, one low – the idea being to use differing levels of resonance. Swap tone. Discuss whether certain contrasting qualities of tone work for different characters. Try another duologue.

3 As in 1 above, but this time each actor should allow vocal tone to slowly transform during the scene, e.g. from soft to hard. This is one of the transformations which can occur spontaneously in response to emotional state – when the speaker is feeling threatened for example.

section 5: **speech**

Voice then is the sound that you make. Speech is how you control the sound, converting it into words. Speech in theatre generally carries much of the important information required by an audience. As such it is absolutely central to the job of acting.

Actors use speech to communicate important information, not just about the story of the play, but about the personality of their character.

In this Section you will be introduced to four new Tools to help you become a more sophisticated communicator and a more versatile actor.

Tool Number 13 – Varying the Pace – assesses how speed of speech represents an often overlooked characteristic of personality and how varying pace of speech can have important effects.

Tool Number 14 – Changing Accent – examines one of the most popular methods of altering character and offers tips on how to develop expertise in using accents.

Tool Number 15 – Focus on Diction – underlines the importance of clear diction for actors

Tool Number 16 – Employing Specials – walks you through some of the most common speech variations with advice on how they can be achieved.

Once again, we'll look first at what each term means. We'll consider what knowledge is required to be able to change each variable and the psychological reasons for variations between people, then I'll end with some suggested speech exercises. As before, you should use your digital recorder liberally.

Speech then has four key variable characteristics: **P**ace, **A**ccent, **D**iction, and what I've called '**S**pecials'. Together they form the mnemonic '**PADS**'. If you put together the variable characteristics of body, voice and speech, you have the mnemonic phrase **THOSE LINT PADS**. Odd though the phrase may be, it works well as an aide-memoire for all the things a transformational character actor can change. If you want to be a versatile character actor, *use those lint pads*.

Tool No. 13: Varying the Pace

Pace describes simply the speed at which speech takes place. As with most personal characteristics, pace of speech is something which we only really notice if there's something irritating about it – something harmful to speech communication. The two obvious extremes are speech so rapid that the listener is unable to keep up and speech so slow that it becomes frustrating to listen to. Usefully, some digital recorders allow you (without linking to a computer) to alter the speed of your recording without altering vocal pitch. This can be valuable (and amusing) when you're exploring pace.

Different speeds of speech create different perceptions of the speaker. Fast speech can suggest confidence, quick-wittedness, spontaneity, energy. Slow speech can suggest reticence, low intelligence, cautiousness, listlessness. But fast speech can also suggest nervousness, and slow speech can be the sign of a confident person who chooses to dictate the pace of communication.

As we explored earlier, people hide things. The nervous person will try to seem confident and in control. The naturally enthusiastic person may try to hide their enthusiasm in order to seem cool. Both illusions can be achieved by altering the pace of speech.

It's really valuable for an actor to have an awareness of pace. One of the challenges of acting, especially in a full-length theatre production, is to maintain an audience's attention throughout the arc of the play. A good story will keep them listening, but you – as a key communicator of the story – shoulder much of the responsibility for keeping them really interested. And an awareness of pace of speech is a valuable, and underused, weapon in the fight to remain interesting.

Of course, you shouldn't ever change pace simply to remain interesting. Pace of speech is a reflection of a person's mental and emotional state so at any point in your character's journey through a play there will be a pace of speech which is appropriate. Don't over-prepare by trawling through your script to plan pace of speech. Understand your character's journey through the play and then in rehearsal do those crucial things which actors must do – keep focused, stay relaxed, listen – and you'll find that your pace of speech shifts spontaneously in reaction to your character's circumstances. Of course it follows that the speed at which you deliver a line may well alter in response to the performance of your fellow-actor.

The best acting performances have an organic quality about them, by which I mean that the actor maintains a psychological and emotional responsiveness, which alters their performance each time. In order to develop the skills needed to let go, and in order to achieve confidence in allowing things like your pace of speech to change spontaneously, you will need to practise in everyday life. You will of course need excellent diction. Once you've mastered clear speech, the full range of variations in pace of speech is open to you.

Let's take a simple question – 'Are you waiting for someone?' – and let's analyse it for a moment, setting its usage within an imagined context. You're in a bar or a cafe, seated beside an attractive stranger. You lack confidence in your ability to approach people, but you don't want to appear nervous. First comes the voice. LINT: Loudness, Inflection, Note, and Tone. Your voice is going to be quite loud, partly because there's background noise, and partly because you're nervous and lack a degree of control. You've been silently practising this question in your head for the last two minutes. You want to sound relaxed but interested so your inflection will be a bit varied. You hope that the notes you use will be close to your true root note. You may use higher notes if you're too nervous. You'd like your tone to be fairly relaxed, not too hard. But your body has other ideas. Your chest and throat are a bit tight, making it feel as if your voice is centred at the back of your throat where you can feel a lot of tension.

Now to speech – in this case, pace of speech. Not too fast, not too slow. You want to make a good impression, you want to sound relaxed:

'waitinfosomeone?'

The point I'm re-stating, which applies to all eight characteristics of voice and speech, as well as all five characteristics of physical behaviour, is that variations occur as a direct result of a person's emotional and psychological state of mind. On a good day, you'll be able to come up with a way of delivering a line which is truthful, interesting and instinctive. On a bad day you'll sound truthful, and will be interesting and apparently instinctive. If you're a good actor no-one will ever know the difference.

One more thing to do with pace. In everyday conversation, people vary pace of speech, but they also vary the length of the pauses between the speaking. Someone who is aggressive will typically pause only very briefly in a conversation – indeed they may continually interrupt the other person. A passive or defensive person may pause for some seconds before speaking. It's not difficult to think of psychological reasons why pausing between speech can alter massively from moment to moment – that's real life.

Acting tips

When you, the actor, are presented with a piece of text in which two characters take turns to speak, it can be easy to forget this simple truth about pauses. You learn your lines, you learn your cues, and then you rehearse with the other actor. If you're focused and confident (and if you know your lines and your cues really well) you can let go and discover by instinct how the pauses between the lines should occur. But if anything goes wrong – if either of you have a reason to be tense – then one or both of you will lose the ability to listen and react, which is the essence of good duologue work. What often follows is that the pausing between the lines of text becomes uniform and therefore predictable. I speak – you pretend to listen and react; you speak – I pretend to listen and react. Good actors who get caught in this situation fall back on instinct and make some alteration in the pausing between lines. Lesser actors very quickly become uninteresting.

One way of overcoming this problem is to employ the analogy of a game of tennis. In tennis, each player has the potential to play a shot from the baseline, from the net, or from somewhere in between. A tennis match played entirely long distance (where both players stay back beyond the baseline, hoping the other will make a mistake) can be really dull to watch. And while no tennis match is ever played solely at the net, a rally at the net can be really exciting. In a typical match both players alter position frequently and suddenly – hanging back at the baseline one moment, rushing the net at the next. And one of the most exhilarating shots to watch is the long-distance lob, which leaves the opponent stranded or lunging for a return. For an actor then the pacing to avoid is the predictable long-distance baseline delivery which has the same rhythm and length of pause each time. The close-net rally is a brief and frantic exchange of words packed with interruptions. The rest of the scene sees each actor continue to vary pace and pauses according to their own psychological state, which shifts from moment to moment. And the lob? Well, that's the devastating one-liner (statement or question) which leaves the receiver stranded.

The following exercises are quite technical. I'd suggest you use them only to help you to get to grips with pacing and pauses.

Exercises: Solo

1 Below is a section of text from Charles Dickens' novel *A Christmas Carol*. Read it aloud now at a normal pace of speech, using your digital recorder to record your own voice.

External heat and cold had little influence on Scrooge. No warmth could warm, no wintry weather chill him.

No wind that blew was bitterer than he, no falling snow was more intent upon its purpose, no pelting rain less open to entreaty.

Foul weather didn't know where to have him.

Nobody ever stopped him in the street to say, with gladsome looks, 'My dear Scrooge, how are you? When will you come to see me?'

No beggars implored him to bestow a trifle, no children asked him what it was o'clock, no man or woman ever once in all his life inquired the way to such and such a place, of Scrooge.

Even the blind men's dogs appeared to know him; and when they saw him coming on, would tug their owners into doorways and up courts; and then would wag their tails as though they said, 'No eye at all is better than an evil eye, dark master!'

Now mark the script in pencil, using the numbers from one to five to represent pace of speech. If you think a pause is appropriate, write in the letter P (a big P for a longer pause, a small p for a short one). Think of your voice in terms of gears. First gear is very slow, fifth gear is very fast indeed. Make sure, above all, that your choice of numbers makes psychological sense from a storyteller's point of view. Record this version on your digital recorder. Play back the two versions for comparison – the one read at your normal pace and this latest one. Try recording it again, altering the pattern of gear changes.

2 This time use a monologue from a play. Go through the speech, marking any changes of pace you feel would occur in response to the character's psychology. Ask yourself questions about the character: is this a difficult thing to say? Does my character mean what they say on this bit or are they masking something? How do they feel towards the listener? Use a pencil with an eraser – you'll find that your choices change. When you've planned delivery of the speech, record it.

3 This exercise invites you to apply random choices of pace which can sometimes lead to really interesting discoveries. You'll need a die and a pencil, and a second monologue which you've divided into small sections. Toss the die. Working from the start of the speech, note down a number for each small section. Use numbers one to five as before. If you throw a six, this is speech so fast that you can barely say the words. Now record the speech, varying pace as planned at random. Listen to the recording and ask, are there moments where the change of pace as speech is unexpectedly effective?

Exercises: Partnered

1 Repeat exercises 2 and 3 above, but this time use duologues. Again, record your work and play it back. As you listen to it, reflect on any new discoveries regarding use of pace.

2 Exercise using the tennis analogy: a duologue. Select a short duologue from a play which you know well. The scene should be naturalistic in style and should allow for multiple interpretations. (Harold Pinter's *The Dumb Waiter* and David

Mamet's *Oleanna* are good examples.) Discuss an inter-pretation of the scene which makes psychological sense for each character: you should try to identify what it is that each of your characters wants from the other. (We'll be going into this in detail in the next Section.) Now run the scene, imagining the two characters as baseline players, i.e. they each pause before responding to the other. Then reassess the scene so that it can be played at the net, i.e. with quick-fire dialogue and your characters often inter-rupting each other. Now mix it up. Then mix it up again. Discuss how different interpretations affect your feelings towards the other actor's character.

3) Repeat exercise 2, this time playing a game for real. At its simplest this could be playing catch facing your partner. At its most complex you could even play tennis (or at least table tennis), speeding up or slowing down the game – and your delivery of the lines – as you feel appropriate.

Tool No. 14: Changing Accent

Believe it or not, you have an accent – everyone does. No one is accentless. The most a person can claim is that their accent does not tie them to a specific geographical region, but rather to a social class – for example the traditionally middle-class English Received Pronunciation (RP) accent. Accents other than RP typically link you to a specific geographical region.

Learning a new accent generally requires a huge amount of time, study and effort. It certainly helps if you're willing to learn the Phonetic Alphabet – that is, the alphabet of sounds which is used in dictionaries to help with pronunciation (see Further Reading). It follows that you need a good ear. You can still work as an actor if accents are not your strong point – the two famous Seans, Connery and Bean, seem to have managed pretty well – but if you want to be fully versatile, you do need a good ear and you need to practise using it.

This section is not an attempt to teach you how to do specific accents. Instead, I offer something which I hope is just as useful: a clear insight into how accents vary. Certain patterns recur and a knowledge of these patterns will take you a long way towards being able to master most accents.

You'll already be familiar with the simple sounds of vowels – the 'a' in cat, the 'e' in hen, and so on. But you should become familiar also with **diphthongs** within speech. A diphthong occurs when one vowel sound slides into another with no consonant in between. Sometimes this switch from one sound to another is very obvious. The word 'boy' is an example of a particularly strong diphthong, which, in standard English, slides from the sound you get in the middle of the word 'good' to the sound you get in the middle of the word 'hit'. (Try it.) But if you analyse it carefully, even such a short word as 'go' represents a diphthong because the pronunciation slides from a sound which is close to the 'u' in the middle of the word 'gun' to a sound which is close to the 'oo' in the middle of the word 'moon' – and this happens almost in an instant. (Try it.) Other diphthongs are found in the centre of the words 'may' and 'hear'.

Diphthong sounds are often the sounds that vary the most from accent to accent. Sometimes a regional accent contains a pronunciation bearing almost no resemblance to the pronunciation of the same sound in RP. This is when it's especially useful to understand diphthongs. Take, for example, the pronunciation of the word 'now' in a Belfast accent. The diphthong in the middle of this word, as it would be spoken in RP, is a sound which slides, approximately, from the sound which you get in the middle of the word 'man' to the sound which you get in the middle of the word 'good'. (Try it.) But when the word 'now' is spoken in a Belfast accent, the diphthong in the middle of the word is totally different. This time, the pronunciation is very close to the diphthong in the word 'boy' (see above). Say out loud the word 'boy', but replace the letter 'b' with the letter 'n'. That's quite close to how different the pronunciation is.

City accents do tend to have certain general characteristics that differ from those within rural, or country, accents. The clichéd image of the country as a quieter, less feverish environment than the noisy, competitive atmosphere of the city is pretty well borne out in practice when it comes to accents. City accents in the UK, such as those from Liverpool, Newcastle, Belfast, and London's East End, tend to have a staccato, broken-up quality. Pace in city accents is generally very quick, and it's often broken up by glottal stopping. Tone tends to be hard. Diction tends to be poor.

Sometimes the most significant difference between individual city accents is in vocal inflection. If you have a good ear you may be able to recognise a few of the major city accents by listening to the inflection pattern alone, without any actual speech. You do though have to be careful with inflection. The accents of Birmingham and Liverpool have fairly similar inflection patterns – non-native speakers often get them mixed up even though there are significant differences in the way specific words are pronounced.

With rural 'country' accents, pace tends to be slower and tone tends to be softer. The inflection pattern in a country accent tends to have a greater musicality: there's often a wider range of notes used. It's as if the slower pace of a rural lifestyle allows people greater freedom to speak without interruption. City accents, by contrast, seem to hint at the speaker's expectation of being interrupted. Compare for example the Belfast Northern Irish accent with a rural Southern Irish accent, and the Glasgow Gorbals accent with a Scottish Highland accent. Compare Cockney with Cornish. In each case the city accent is hard, the rural accent softer.

Acting tips

If you're keen to learn accents, I'd recommend starting some sort of scrapbook. Allocate a page to each specific regional accent. For each one, reflect on the eight key vocal and speech characteristics that vary – i.e. LINT PADS. If you can think of any, include the names of famous people – or friends – who are native speakers of that accent. (In the Appendix you'll find a sample layout, focusing on the Liverpool accent.) It can help to memorise a simple phrase to help you click into a particular accent: for example I use 'alright mate?' to help me quickly adopt a London Cockney accent (it comes out as something like 'aaw-why/may', with a glottal stop in the middle).

Where possible, include recordings of each accent. Some recordings of accents are commercially available, but be aware that poor or dated versions of accents are worse than useless. There are books dedicated to accents that include audio recordings, but remember that, as a general rule, if all the accents are spoken by the same person, mistakes will inevitably be made (one exception to this is Methuen Drama's impressive 'Access Accents' series). Some valuable and free-to-access resources are available online, though these do seem to move or disappear quite quickly, so I plan to maintain live links to the best ones on my own website.

Exercises: Solo

  1 Record your own voice. Just talk about something everyday (what you've done so far today, what you're planning to do later). When you play it back, transcribe a small section of your spoken words onto paper. Leave a gap between lines. Play that small section back again and listen carefully to the vocal inflection. Draw a simple pattern above the words you spoke, which shows how the inflection develops and changes during your speech. If you've ever seen this, it should look like a simple version of a transcription of birdsong. Here's a sentence with an example of a basic transcription of an inflection pattern:

I can't see any reason why I should, I really can't.

Repeat the exercise, but record someone else – ideally someone with a different regional accent. Compare the inflection patterns. Certain accents, such as the Birmingham accent, tend to have simple patterns of inflection that repeat on a bit of a loop. When you've recorded and transcribed the accent, and drawn a pattern for the vocal inflection, mimic the recorded speaker's accent.

2 Take the simple phrase: 'I can't wait until tomorrow – it's my birthday'. Select two accents known to you – one an urban 'city' accent and one a rural 'country' accent. Write the phrase down twice on paper with a big gap in between. Have a go at each accent, allowing yourself to play with vocal variables such as tone. Record your efforts. Repeat the exercise with two more contrasting accents.

3 Listen to a native speaker using their own accent. Mimic out loud what they say and how they say it – you should be repeating the words only a fraction of a second after the speaker. It takes a lot of practice, but it's an excellent way to learn an accent. It's helpful if, at first, you can have a transcription of what the person is about to say. With experience, you can just copy them live.

Tool No. 15: Focus on Diction

Diction means clarity of speech. Good diction means speaking clearly with good articulation while still sounding natural. It's an essential skill for an actor. Audiences seated on the back row of a big theatre auditorium can only gain a limited amount of information from watching your body: it may be impossible to see the subtleties of your facial expressions. In radio drama there is only your voice (and your breath). So how clearly you say what you say is, obviously, central to good communication.

Contemporary actors working in a climate where the appearance of naturalism is crucial face something of a dilemma. In real life, few people have perfect diction. In real life, words spoken in a strong regional accent are often hard to understand. In real life, psychological stress will often lead to less-than-perfect clarity of speech – yet dramas of all sorts tackle the most stressful of moments in the lives of people across the social divide. Here, then, is the dilemma. If you are acting a character who is under heavy emotional stress, which is more important – realistic psychology and an authentic accent or speaking the lines clearly?

Of course, it's not a question of either/or within naturalism. Both are essential. What's required from actors is a skilful blending of two elements – a convincing and appropriate expression of psychology and emotion in an authentic-sounding accent, completed with clear diction that reaches all of the audience all of the time. So concentrate on your acting and add a bit to your diction. So-called **'plosive' sounds** in particular (think of them as explosions), such as p-, d-, k- and g-, need to be hit harder and cleaner than in everyday speech. These plosives also need to be accurately voiced or unvoiced: d- and t- are identical in terms of how they are produced, yet while d- involves added sound delivered by the vocal cords, t- is made voicelessly. This subtle difference can be especially confusing to an audience if the speaker is using an accent. I once taught a student from Finland whose accent inverted the 't' and 'd' sounds so that the word 'debt' came out as 'ted'.

As with other key aspects of voice and speech production (projection for example) there's a great deal of highly informed and accessible literature available to help actors improve their diction (see Further Reading). So, with apologies, I'm not going to dwell further on diction here.

Acting tips

The muscles involved in speech, especially the lips, need to be properly warmed up and actively used so get into the habit of speaking aloud tongue-twisters (see exercise 3 below) and pretending to chew very chewy chewing gum. Also, the parts of the body most-used when producing voice (chest, throat, mouth) and associated muscle areas (such as neck and shoulders) need to be kept as relaxed as possible to avoid strangling the voice with tension and to facilitate good resonance. The vowel and diphthong sounds in words are the sounds which carry the resonance of the voice. As such they are, in a long-distance medium such as theatre, arguably the most important element in transmitting a character's emotional mood: they need to be as unfettered as possible.

In close-up media such as film and television, the viewer expects an intensely realistic style of performance so any technique you use must be invisible. It's probably best not to think too consciously about diction when acting for camera. My advice here is to focus hard on what your character is fighting for and just be mindful not to mumble.

Exercises:

1 Read aloud a section of text from a story (you could use the excerpt from Dickens' *A Christmas Carol* in Solo exercise 1 in the Pace section.) Imagine you're chewing your words like gum. Exaggerate the clarity of your pronunciation by using greater muscularity with your lips, jaw and tongue. Hit the consonants hard but cleanly while working to avoid tension in the throat. Since vowel sounds carry strong resonance and help to express emotion, work consciously to keep your vocal expression as free and relaxed as possible.

2 Repeat exercise 1 but this time speak as quickly as you possibly can and record it. Play it back. How easily can you understand every word? Play it back again, stopping the recording whenever there is a slight lack of clarity. Read other bits of text. Ask someone else to listen to the recordings. Look for a pattern: do you tend to use 'splashy' consonants? Do you tend to 'swallow' certain vowel sounds? Do you use too many glottal stops? When you've seen a pattern, practise altering your diction. Re-record your speech. How clear is it now?

3 Practise daily, and before any performance, these tongue-twisters:

Unique New York, New York unique
A proper cup of coffee in a proper copper coffee pot
A proper crop of poppies is a proper poppy crop
The skunk sat on the stump. The stump thunk the skunk
stunk and the skunk thunk the stump stunk

...and for the ruder-minded:

Mrs Hunt has a square-cut punt. Not a punt cut square, but
a square-cut punt

...and when you become too familiar with them, find and
learn new ones.

4 Find and learn an emotionally-charged monologue from a
play. Spend at least fifteen minutes drawing yourself into an
appropriate psychological state. Perform the piece, recording
it on your digital recorder. Play it back, concentrating only on
your diction. Re-record it with improvements.

5 As exercise 4, but this time perform in a large space so that
you have to cope with projecting your voice using good
diction while retaining an appropriate psychological state.
Leave your digital recorder at a greater distance from you.
Play back the recording, focusing on diction. Re-record it
with improvements.

Tool No. 16: Employing Specials

'Specials' are common idiosyncrasies of speech. Often they're
described as speech defects, but they're not really defects – just
variations from the accepted standard pronunciation of speech.

One common Special occurs when speakers replace the
unvoiced sound 'th' with 'f'. For example, someone will say, 'I
fink so'. This particular Special has long been common practice
for London Cockney speakers; but it's now far more widespread
in the UK, particularly among younger speakers. I find the link

with youth culture interesting because the use of 'f' instead of 'th' is also common among very young children. So perhaps, by choosing not to adopt what might be considered adult RP pronunciation, speakers are rejecting a perceived adult, middle-class culture.

The use of the unvoiced 'f-' instead of the unvoiced 'th-' is echoed in the use of the voiced 'v-' as a replacement for the voiced 'th'. 'Whether', for example, becomes 'wevver'. Note though that this doesn't tend to happen at the start of a word. For example, 'this' would not become 'vis' though it can become 'dis'.

Another Special occurs when people have difficulty pronouncing the strong 'r'. The 'r' is instead pronounced 'w', or on a point somewhere between the two sounds. So the word 'worry' becomes 'wowy'. Again, a mild version of this is a common characteristic of a Cockney accent. It's interesting to note that less muscularity is needed for the Specials mentioned so far, compared to what's needed for the RP version.

Another Special is connected to the pronunciation of the 's' sound. Pronunciation hinges on the position of the tongue, especially the tip. The standard pronunciation is achieved by gently placing the tip of the tongue close to the lower alveolar ridge (this is the gum area at the front of the mouth from which the lower front teeth protrude). If you let the tip of the tongue move away from the alveolar ridge, and in particular if you let the tip come fractionally between the teeth, you start to lisp. The 's' sound starts to become thicker, splashier and, ultimately, like a 'th' sound. The shape of the tongue is also significant. Unsurprisingly, the precision required to create a clean 's' sound means that variations are common.

Another Special occurs when the flow of air is momentarily stopped during speech – the glottal stop. Once again, London Cockney is the UK regional accent within which this Special most frequently occurs, but it's common too in, for example, the Geordie (Newcastle) accent. It's usually a kind of lazy abbreviation: the word 'bottle' loses its central 't' sound and becomes 'bo'l'. Try the phrase 'I've got to get another bottle'. There are at least three glottal stops in that sentence if it's spoken by a Cockney or a Geordie.

If you've realised that your own everyday speech makes use of one or more of these Specials then, as a transformational character actor, you may have a bit of a problem. In particular if you have a strongly non-standard 's' sound, you may struggle to find work in recorded media, especially radio drama and voice-over: somehow a microphone seems to amplify this special characteristic and this can be quite jarring on the listener's ear. So do think about getting some one-to-one tuition with a good speech therapist.

An unconscious tendency to use glottal stops in everday speech can be harmful, too. As discussed earlier such vocal tension is not, as a general rule, good for your voice. In theatre you should in general be aiming for a continuous flow of breath, regulated by your character's thought and feelings. It's easier said than done perhaps but, if you can, use glottal stops sparingly on stage.

If you discover you need further voice or speech training, you should ideally enlist the help of a good voice coach or speech therapist. At the very least you should buy, and use daily, one of the excellent specialist voice and speech books on the market (see Further Reading). The book should break down pronunciation in physical terms, explaining tongue and lip position, for example. Be prepared to start from scratch and work daily on the suggested exercises.

Acting tips

It can make for a really enjoyable challenge to use Specials in your acting. A word or two of warning though: Specials are, by definition, deviations from Received Pronunciation. If you use Specials during speech, you risk harming clear communication. Above all else, your audience needs to hear what you're saying.

And don't make things too hard for yourself. Using Specials requires hard work in the planning and rehearsal stages, and focus during the performance stage. If you're not careful, your audience will be able to see the join – they'll notice something which is arguably not important. Even worse, it can take so much effort to get it right that the truthfulness and spontaneity of your performance may suffer.

Exercises:

1 Start speaking, without any preparation, in your own normal voice. You could just describe what you've done in the last week. As you speak, practise spontaneously converting 'th' into 'f' whenever the sound occurs.

2 As exercise 1, this time converting 'r' into 'w'.

3 As above, this time converting your normal ' s' sound into a thicker, lisping 's' sound by minutely protruding your tongue through your teeth. Move the position of your tongue again and discover what other 's' sounds you can create.

4 As above, this time watching out for opportunities to use glottal stops. Speak slowly at first, then repeat words and phrases which seem to lend themselves to the use of glottal stops. To begin with try out a London Cockney accent. After that try it with your own, and with other, accents.

5 Imagine you are making a video to join a dating agency. Talk about yourself and, as you speak, try altering pronunciation in all three of the areas mentioned above.

6 As in 5, but this time use a monologue from a serious playscript and get someone to be an outside eye. Ask them at the end how your changed delivery affected their view of your character.

This section is exlusively to do with what goes on inside you – thoughts, emotions, sensations, memories – all linked as they are to the conscious and subconscious mind. We're going to explore how an actor can use knowledge, skill and imagination to create a sense of inner reality during rehearsal and performance.

Actors use emotion and imagination to varying degrees depending on their preferred style of acting (e.g. Storyteller or Inhabiter); on the working methods of their director; and on the training they have received. Work on the inner life of a character can be highly rewarding, not least because it's here that truly spontaneous discoveries are most likely to occur.

In this Section we'll be adding the final four new Tools to your repertoire, all of which are forged from the teachings of Stanislavski.

Tool Number 17 – The Magic What If? – explores that most basic yet powerful of mental activities: the act of stimulating your imagination.

Tool Number 18 – Energising your Character – examines the benefits of mapping your character's psychological journey through a play, using objectives, barriers and possible actions.

Tool Number 19 – Imagining Sensations – discusses the importance of sensory awareness in performance and considers how this can best be developed.

Tool Number 20 – Generating Emotion – analyses the importance of stimulating emotion using psychological spurs such as revisited memories.

Once, when I was rehearsing the role of twin Eddie for a tour of Willy Russell's *Blood Brothers*, I inexplicably found that I was crying – sobbing, actually. In the scene the seven-year-old Eddie was saying goodbye to Mrs Johnstone, a woman who (unbeknownst to Eddie) happened to be his natural mother, something clicked inside me and, in a room full of actors and stage management crew, I found I was sobbing like a baby (or rather, like a seven-year-old child). In subsequent rehearsals this never happened again, but the memory of that emotional outburst always stayed with me, and with the actor playing Mrs Johnstone, so that the scene forever retained a sense of childish loss as its undercurrent.

In the previous Sections of this book we've gone into considerable detail exploring what behavioural signs are there for you to recognise and use. These things – and in particular THOSE LINT PADS – give you, the actor, a huge repertoire from which to draw as part of your task of telling stories about the human-imal. It's no accident that this Inner Life section comes last. You should now be pretty fully versed in the outward expression of the inner life of a person. Remember, too, that we've already explored the psychological reasons why people's behaviour changes in each of the THOSE LINT PADS areas.

You'll notice a slight change in format in this final Section. The Acting Tips have been incorporated into the main text simply because we're now looking specifically at the skill of acting (so you could say that everything you're about to read represents Acting Tips). Also, each sub-section now includes exercises and activities within the text, rather than at the end. This means that as a reader you can exercise your imagination as you go along, which better suits the spirit of this Section. After all, as you sit, seemingly innocently reading this Section, how many of the people nearby know what you're *really* up to? There really is a minefield in this area. Views are polarised and intense. In one corner are those who believe that inner life is the single most important aspect of acting. Here you'll be likely to find Lee Strasberg, Michael Chekhov and Konstantin Stanislavski, and in support, acting greats such as Marlon Brando, Robert De Niro, Daniel Day Lewis and Al Pacino. In the other corner are the advocates of what we might call Representational acting – acting which seems real but does not require constant and intense emotional experience to be effective. Here we might find Laurence Olivier, Michael Caine, Dame Judi Dench – and a younger version of Konstantin Stanislavski. Even Brando, preparing for his *Godfather* role with cotton wool tucked inside his cheeks, seems to occupy a more central position along with Anthony Hopkins.

So who is right? Neither side? Both sides? It's surely a matter of opinion. But I do believe this: technique and instinct should always be working together. Blending these two things so that you can't see the join is, for me, the essence of great acting.

So I'm going to focus on offering some ideas on exploring the inner life of a character. As ever, they mostly spring from the mind of Stanislavski. He recognised (and experienced) the need for actors to have a practical process to help them overcome the inherent unreality of acting: the requirement to act on cue between, say, 7.30pm and 10pm; the demand to do so nightly for perhaps as long as a year using the same words every time; and the unremitting falseness of a situation whereby you stand on a stage trying to ignore both your audience and the Assistant Stage Manager perched in the wings.

Tool No. 17: The Magic What If?

The final key to keeping your acting as truthful as possible is, of course, active use of your imagination. Interestingly, active imagining is used a lot these days by those other performers who work under heavy psychological and physical pressure – e.g.

professional sportsmen and women. Sprinters and tennis players use it (though they may call it visualisation). They visualise that moment when they reach the tape in first place or when they deliver a match-winning first-serve ace. And it works (usually).

Actors imagine too, of course. It's at the very heart of what they do. To be a good actor, you need to be open and responsive to your imagination. Stanislavski's most simple concept was also I think his most effective – the so-called 'Magic If'. *What if – ?* This simple phrase is a wonderfully direct challenge to the part of you that enjoyed playing games of imagination as a child. In *An Actor Prepares*, Stanislavski sets up a hugely powerful 'what if' which locates the threat of a deranged would-be killer just outside the room. Wherever you are as you read this, imagine that now you (not a character, but the real you) are at risk of attack from a person nearby who has the means to kill you. What do you feel? What, specifically, is your new main emotion?

Rather cleverly, that no longer becomes the key issue. Infinitely more important is the question, 'What do I do?' How do you ensure your survival? What about loved ones nearby? What can you do to protect them? What if the would-be killer hasn't seen you? If you keep still they may just go away. Use your imagination now to focus hard on that. As you do so, your mind will be whirring with thoughts and feelings, but your body will be pretty well still. You will be experiencing **inner life**.

Of course, you don't have to be still to experience inner life. Indeed, Section Three of this book explored in some detail how even minor tensions and movements give out clues. You should have learned, through that earlier Section on the body, what the external signs of a person's thoughts and feelings are. What we're considering now is how an imagined stimulus (an image or a memory, for example) can spur you on to physical action. We're now going inside the character to discover how things you imagine while in character help to prompt a spontaneous physical expression.

Back to the deranged would-be killer for a moment. You're keeping as still as possible in the hope that they won't see you and will go away. You just want them to go away. What are you feeling? Who cares, frankly. You just want them to go away. But they're still there, edging around, peering in your direction. You hear a shout or a bang. Have they seen you? If they have, what now? You need an escape route. How well do you know this place? How far is it to safety and help? Would it be safer to sit it out and try to reason with them? How are you feeling? (Not great, you think, but can we discuss that later?)

Life isn't always that dramatic, of course – though in truth you face a similar challenge when you're hurrying somewhere and you find yourself on a crash-course towards an irritating person you really want to avoid. And though they're not threatening to kill you, they may inadvertently bore you to death. Look again at the questions in the paragraph above – they still apply. If you're in company now as you're reading this, select someone nearby as a person you desperately want to avoid (you'll need to invent a reason that relates to your social relationship with them). Keep your physical movement as minimal as possible and concentrate hard on what action you will take if they approach you.

Something which Stanislavski bravely asserted, and which I've hinted at in the scenarios described above, is that emotions are not things that you should ever plan in advance. Being able to act intense emotions on cue is sometimes seen as the mark of a great actor, but, in truth, while such acting can at best be very moving, at worst it can be an unwelcome party trick that simply detracts from the story of the play.

Still, it's tempting (and common practice) to map out a character's progress through a play by trying to pin down changing emotions. You think to yourself, 'I'll be angry at this point' or 'I was amused before but now my character's getting upset'. Resist. If you build a performance from predetermined emotions, your acting will become generalised, predictable and unresponsive to the other actors. And you set yourself up to fail ('damn, I didn't cry on that bit AGAIN!'). Look at Hamlet. In his story he spends much of his time failing to act – he keeps discovering or inventing reasons why he should hold back. It's tempting to label him as depressed, bitter – even suicidal. But play him that way and after two hours your audience will be egging him on to do it. Better instead to acknowledge Shakespeare's talent for creating believable and sophisticated characters who act in response to their changing circumstances, and to work out what Hamlet is thinking. After all, who told the grieving Hamlet that his uncle murdered his father? A ghost, that's who. I don't know about you, but I'd need a bit more to go on before killing my uncle – especially if he's making an effort to be nice to me. I'd need to do some soul-searching and some corroborative digging. For you, the actor, presented only with a script made up of dialogue, you will need to engage in some active imagining in order to breathe life into your character's psychology.

If active imagining is so important for actors, how then can you develop your imagination? Simple: practice. Play 'what if – ?' games as you go about your daily business, and especially when you're bored (when your mind is looking for a stimulus). Where should you start? Wherever you like. You could though do worse than revisiting some of the Exercises in earlier sections of this book and adding a powerful 'what if – ?' to each scenario.

Example: Natasha from *Three Sisters*

Read and rehearse this longer scene below from Act Three. For this scene to work fully for both actors and audience, there should initially be a strong sense of imminent threat (from fire, which has been sweeping through the town). The stress of this situation doubtless contributes to Natasha losing her temper so violently later in the scene and to other characters showing their true feelings too. As actors rehearsing the scene, you could start by asking, 'What if, while we were running the scene, there was a genuine threat of fire outside the building?' Try alternatives. Have you ever been in a place where there was a threat of natural disaster or terrorism? If so, try to recall the detail of that experience, what you wanted, what you actually did. Add it to the mix as you imagine the fire. If not, well, it is a magic if. Be as focused as possible – and imagine it.

[NATASHA comes in.]

NATASHA

They say we urgently need a committee to help the fire victims. What do you think? It's an excellent idea. The poor need help, it's the duty of the rich. Bobik and little Sophie are sleeping on as if nothing's happened. There are so many people here, the place is full of them. There's an outbreak of flu in the town. I'm so frightened the children will catch it.

OLGA *[Not listening]*

You can't see the fire in this room, it's quiet in here.

NATASHA

Yes ... I suppose I'm a mess. *[At the mirror]* They say I'm putting on weight ... it's not true! It's not. Masha's fast asleep; the poor thing's worn out. *[Coldly, to ANFISA]* How dare you sit in my presence! Get up! Go on, get out! *[Exit ANFISA; a pause]* I have no idea why you keep that old woman on.

OLGA *[Confused]*

I'm sorry, I don't understand ...

NATASHA

She's no use here. She came from the countryside, she should go back to it ... Spoiling her, I call it! I must have order in the house. We don't want anyone useless here. *[Strokes Olga's cheek]* You're tired, poor thing! Our head-mistress is tired! And when my little Sophie starts school I shall be so afraid of you.

OLGA

I shan't be headmistress.

NATASHA

They're going to appoint you, Olga. It's settled.

OLGA

Then I'll refuse the job. I can't ... I'm not strong enough ... *[Drinks water]* You were so rude to nanny just now ... I'm sorry. I can't stand it ... it all feels so dark around me ...

NATASHA *[Alarmed]*

Forgive me, Olga, please forgive me ... I didn't mean to upset you.

[MASHA gets up, grabs a pillow and storms out.]

OLGA

Remember, dear ... perhaps we had an unconventional upbringing, but I can't bear this. Such behaviour really affects me, it makes me ill ... gets me down ...

NATASHA

Forgive me, forgive me ... *[Kisses her.]*

OLGA

Even the least rudeness upsets me.

NATASHA

I often say too much, it's true, but you must agree, dear, that she could just as easily go back to the country.

OLGA

She's been with us for thirty years.

NATASHA

But she can't work any more. Either I don't understand, or you don't want to understand me. She's no good for working – all she can do is sleep or sit around.

OLGA

Then let her sit around.

NATASHA *[Surprised]*

What do you mean? She's a servant. *[becoming distressed]* I don't understand you, Olga. I've got a nurse, a wet-nurse, we have a cook, a housemaid ... what do we want that old woman for as well? What good is she?

[Fire siren is heard]

OLGA

I've aged ten years tonight.

NATASHA

We have to agree on this, Olga. Your place is at the school, mine – in the home. You're devoted to your teaching, I am to the household. So if I speak of servants I know what I'm talking about; I do know what I am talking about ... And tomorrow there'll be nothing more from that old thief, that old hag ... *[Stamping]* that witch! And don't you dare to upset me! Don't you dare! *[Stopping short]* Really, if you don't move downstairs, we're just going to keep on arguing. This is terrible.

[Enter KULIGIN, MASHA's husband]

KULIGIN

Where's Masha? We have to go home. The fire seems to be dying down. *[Stretches himself]* Only one block has been destroyed, but there's been such a wind I thought the whole town might burn down. *[Sits]* I'm exhausted. My dear Olga ... I often think if it hadn't been for Masha I'd have married you. You're so lovely ... I'm utterly worn out. *[Listens.]*

OLGA

What is it?

KULIGIN

Our doctor's been drinking hard; he's terribly drunk. Perhaps he did it on purpose! *[Gets up]* I think he's coming ... Can you hear him? Yes, there ... *[Laughs]* What a man ... really ... I'm going to hide. *[Goes to the cupboard and stands in the corner]* What a rogue.

OLGA

He didn't touch a drop for two years, and then he suddenly goes and gets blind drunk ...

[Retires with NATASHA to the back of the room.]

Tool No. 18: Energising Your Character

Units and objectives

At any given moment in a well-written play a character is up to something. It's what characters do to keep busy, to fill out their lives. (People, of course, are just the same.) In a play, it's what keeps the story moving forward.

Often the thing a character wants is hidden among the lines and the action; you need to do some detective work. Sometimes the want is straightforward and explicit. Here's a moment from the provocative play *Blue/Orange* by Joe Penhall. Bruce, a doctor, is meeting with Christopher, diagnosed with Borderline Personality Disorder. Christopher believes he is about to be released back into the community.

BRUCE

Relax.

CHRISTOPHER

I should relax and calm myself.

BRUCE
Take a few breaths. Would you like some water?

CHRISTOPHER *(fidgeting)*
Uh?

BRUCE
Would you like a cup of water?

CHRISTOPHER
Coke.

BRUCE
No, you can't have –

CHRISTOPHER
Ice-cold Coke. The Real Thing.

BRUCE
No, you know you can't have Coke –

CHRISTOPHER
Yeah I can because –

BRUCE
What did I tell you about Coke?

CHRISTOPHER
I'm going home tomorrow.

BRUCE
What's wrong with drinking Coke?

CHRISTOPHER
But I'm going home.

BRUCE

> Chris? Come on you know this, it's important. What's wrong with Coke?

Pause.

CHRISTOPHER

> It rots your teeth.

BRUCE

> No – well, yes – and...? What else does it do to you?

CHRISTOPHER

> Makes my head explode.

BRUCE

> Well – no – no – what does it do to you really?

CHRISTOPHER

> Makes my head explode – oh man – I know – I get you.

BRUCE

> It's not good for you, is it?

CHRISTOPHER

> No. It's bad.

For once then we have a short sequence in which it's obvious what a character is fighting for: Christopher wants his drink of Coke. It's less clear, however, what Bruce wants from Christopher.

But circumstances change. The way in which a character's circumstances change, and how your character responds to the changes, energises your character within the story of the play. Follow these changes carefully and you will create a useable actor's map for planning your character's journey. Stanislavski's solution – another brilliantly simple device – was to divide up the play into small sections, or units, in which an actor's character is fighting for something specific. This 'want' he called an **Objective**.

To map out the units in a play, go back first to your Character Profile Sheet and identify (or remind yourself) what is your character's **Lifetime Objective**. Look again, too, at their **Favourite Fantasy**. Lodge these two elements in your mind as you move to the next stage. Pretty well everything you come up with should be somehow connected with your character's desire for those two lifetime goals.

Next, go through your script from the start of the play, marking your script in pencil each time there is some significant change in circumstances. Often this means that a character in the story enters or leaves, but it can also mean that one character has started to push for something new within the scene. Every time something significant changes, there's an effect on the characters in the scene. If someone enters, you have to make an instant assessment of how to react to their presence. Should you greet them, do you need to ask them something, do you want them to go away, or what? If someone leaves, what does that mean for you? You can then perhaps relax and re-think your plans; you can talk about them now they're gone. Perhaps you have just lost an important ally and need a new strategy. Each provocation must have a reaction. The same is true for the more subtle changes. If your character is trying to persuade another character to sit and they do sit, then you've got what you wanted so you'll naturally move on to the next thing you want. If your character is failing to persuade the other character to sit, what do you do? It may be that you try a different tack to get them to sit in which case you're still in the same unit. Or you may give up and fight for something new, which means that your next unit has begun.

Once you've identified the units, number them from one upwards. (I tend to identify an average of two or three per page, but they can vary from a tiny unit which takes place before anyone speaks to perhaps two pages of intensive dialogue.) After that, the process is essentially quite simple and is certainly instinctive. You view each unit from each character's perspective, then you get inside your own character's heart and head to find out what they are up to. When you've found each discrete 'want' – your character's objective in each unit – lodge it firmly in your own heart and mind, remembering it always with the phrase 'I want ...'. A word of advice – don't be vague. Make each objective specific and playable. 'I want you to like me' is vague and hard to play. 'I want to make you smile' is specific and suggests actions you might take to achieve it. Also, be instinctive when deciding when a unit changes – this is not a science. If you think you may have changed unit numbers too soon, well, that's why you're using a pencil. And anyway Unit 15 could easily vanish or be split into Units 15a and 15b at a later point. If you're not sure if there's a change in unit, let the unit continue.

Do this with a small section of a play and you have a short series of specific objectives to fight for, and a focus for your energies onstage. Do this with the full script and you will have sketched out a simple psychological map to follow throughout the whole journey of the play.

Barriers

Of course it's all very well wanting something, but what if you don't get it? Life, it's been said, is what happens to us when we're busy making other plans. So it is with characters. If things are getting in the way, then the presence of an obstacle can in itself be fascinating. If you're reading this sitting among other people, pick someone nearby and secretly imagine the objective 'I want to kiss you'. Assuming that (for now at least) you have to settle for less, then your struggle – the sense that things are getting in the way – can give your acting real focus.

The things that get in the way are quite simply **'Barriers'**. Barriers can be real, physical barriers – Juliet longs for Romeo ('Come, Romeo!'), but as far as she can tell he's simply not there so the barrier is the seemingly vast distance between them. Then there are psychological barriers (Hamlet's only source of clues as to who killed his father is his dead father).

It's important not to gloss over this barrier aspect of a character's inner life. I'm all for actors imagining things beyond the lines and the stage directions – anything that helps you believe in your character's given circumstances can surely only be positive. Just thinking it, though, doesn't mean that the audience sense it too. But when you translate what you're thinking and feeling into an active 'want' – when you make an active effort to achieve an objective – then that battle for something you want is a thing the audience can observe and can try to understand. The process of playing a character's active objective represents the crucial link between what you're thinking and feeling, and what your audience can witness. And the barriers raise the stakes. When audiences see people struggling to achieve something, it pulls harder on their sense of empathy. By making imaginative use of objectives and barriers, you're acting with focus and truthfulness, actively telling the story of the play, and doing so while staying fully in character.

Let's imagine for a moment that you're not reading a book, but are listening to me give a lecture. We're in a classroom which contains me, you and a dozen or so other acting students. (You decide the time and place, and we'll both decide who the people are in the group.)

The subject of the lecture is 'Objectives and Barriers'. I've spoken the words above out loud – the ones which begin after the headline 'Energising your character'. You're keen to learn (or refresh) and I'm keen to share the knowledge.

Let's add some details to spice things up.

I'm here as a guest lecturer and this is the first time we've been in class together so although I've taken a register I don't yet know your name. You learned a bit about objectives from a favourite teacher a year ago, but didn't fully grasp it. There was a party last night and some of the other acting students in the room are trying to hide the after-effects: three who were at the party are absent. You can vaguely hear singing in a neighbouring room, a recent song from the charts.

Let's think through the possible consequences of these new given circumstances.

I want to teach you want to learn. But three of your fellow actors didn't even turn up today. I know this, because I've marked them absent on my workshop register. So no matter how keen I am to teach them, their absence is a solid physical barrier to me achieving this. I can leave notes for them – they could even watch a video of the lecture – but I've no guarantee that notes will be read or video watched so, as far as those three are concerned, I've failed in my goal.

Another student actor is suffering a physical barrier because English is his second language and he's having trouble under-standing my accent and my fast pace of speech (I'm a bit nervous). The actor could ask me to slow down, but he's embar-rassed at his own sense of inadequacy so he keeps quiet. His embarrassment is a psychological barrier which prevents him from learning. Anyway, he was at the lecture given by your favourite teacher a year ago and he felt he'd grasped the concepts well. That teacher had referred to obstacles rather than barriers, which now seems confusing, so this student with limited English has decided to stick with his prior knowledge and switch off in class, while politely pretending to listen.

I, meanwhile, as an experienced teacher, have noticed that this student is showing signs of what I'm labelling NDS – Nodding Dog Syndrome. Whatever I say, as soon as our eyes meet he nods reassuringly. I know there's a possible problem but without knowing the group better I don't know what the problem is. I decide to go over the main points of the lecture again in brief so that everyone can take something away from the class. As soon as I do so I sense that one of the more engaged listeners has mentally dropped out and I may struggle to get her back. Mean-while the singer in the next room continues to sing the recent chart song loud enough for us all to hear. To me, the singing is an annoying physical barrier – I have to raise my voice to compete. To you, it's a psychological barrier – the song reminds you of something special which happened during your last holiday.

Examples of both physical and psychological barriers can be found pretty well at any point in any play. I'd suggest though that you don't write them in to your script – yet. Barriers can often be things which only reveal themselves when you're actually on your feet running the scene. Let's say you've mapped out the units and come up with an objective – a 'want' – at the start of each unit. Next, have a go at trying out a few units. Fight for each objective as it changes. Where are the problems? New ones may present themselves. 'I can't say this to my friend because that person by the door can hear too.' 'I want her to go but she's already taking her coat off.' 'I want him to smile but he's not even looking at me.'

A word of warning – as an acting student put it to me recently:

> 'I can see the value of Objectives and Barriers, but what if the Objective is so challenging that you simply can't commit to it? What if your Objective is, say, to tell someone their father has died?'

It strikes me that the task of passing on such serious news is an obligation – a duty – rather than a desire. In this situation you may choose to look at things from a different perspective. Perhaps every atom in your body yearns for a strong black coffee or a hug from your partner or simply an escapist snooze, yet it has fallen to you to pass on the terrible news. Here, I would argue, the giving of bad news is a barrier to your keener ambition rather than the objective itself.

Units, Objectives and Barriers – an exercise

Here's a bit of dialogue from earlier in this book. Re-read it now, and see if you can identify any changes in unit, any objectives, any physical barriers and/or any psychological barriers. I've written the dialogue to be intentionally vague so you can apply more than one interpretation to it:

A: Hello.

B: Hello.

A: Cold, isn't it?

B: It is.

A: Have we met before?

B: Have we? I don't know.

A: I think we have.

B: When?

A: I don't know.

Here's one possible deconstruction of the interaction. Read it through once, then try playing each character:

A park bench. B, who is attractive and has a non-native style of dress, is seated at one end. B is listening to music via earphones.

Unit 1:

A approaches B and sits.

A first wants to know if B speaks English.

Physical barrier = B is listening to music and can't hear.

Psychological barrier = B is also showing subtle non-verbal communication which indicates a desire for privacy.

B wants to be left alone to think.

Physical barrier = A has just sat on the end of the bench.

Psychological barrier = B has been brought up to be polite to strangers.

A: *(leaning into view, loudly)* Hello.

B: *(removing earphones while turning very slightly away from A)* Hello.

Unit 2:

A wants eye contact with B.

Physical barrier = B is now turned slightly further away.

Psychological barrier = B's slight turn has dented A's confidence

B wants still to be left alone.

Physical barrier = A is still there.

Psychological barrier = A's voice sounds friendly & attractive

A: Cold, isn't it?

B: It is.

A: Have we met before?

B: Have we? *(at last B turns to look at A)* I don't know.

Unit 3:

A wants to make B smile. No physical barrier.

Psychological barrier = B seems shy of full eye contact

B still wants to be left alone.

Physical barrier = A is still there.

Psychological barrier = A looks attractive

A: I think we have.

B: When?

A: *(pulling an expression that says, 'My memory is hopeless!')* I don't know.

B: *(smiling)* No.

What I've added into the scene are simply some of the thoughts and desires that drive each of the two characters in the small section shown. It might look a bit daunting – I've added quite a lot of background. But it doesn't have to be as detailed as that. Here's an abbreviated version, which just the actor playing A might use:

A park bench.

Unit 1:

(Sit on end)

(Ob = 'B – speak!'. Phys B = music. Psych B = 'alone' body lang.)

A: Hello.

B: Hello.

Unit 2:

(Obj = 'look at me!' Phys B = B turned away. Psych B = I'm losing confidence)

A: Cold, isn't it?

B: It is.

A: Have we met before?

B: Have we? I don't know.

Unit 3:

(Obj = 'smile!' Psych B = I'm shy re eye contact)

A: I think we have.

B: When?

A: I don't know. *(show jokey 'hopeless memory!')*

B: No.

So you can still plan your map of Units/Objectives/Barriers without drowning in words. Simply work out each of your character's specific objectives, physical barriers, and psychological barriers at each point in the play, and you'll be well on your way to a focused performance. Apply that knowledge bravely but sensitively in rehearsal, and be open to changes (keep using a pencil). You'll be writing yourself a map for a secure first night.

Incidentally, if you're thinking that a full three units in the space of ten lines is quite a lot, it's worth noting that the circumstances in a scene do basically dictate the number of units. One last look at the lines. This time, the scenario is that B is happily reading, while A approaches simply thinking that they recognise B:

Unit 1

> *A wants to know if B is an acquaintance from some years ago.*

> *Physical barrier = B's face is hard to see as B is reading*

> *Psychological barrier = A thinks they may have made a mistake.*

> *B wants to carry on reading. No physical barrier.*

> *Psychological barrier is that A seems to want to talk.*

A: Hello.

B: Hello.

A: Cold, isn't it?

B: It is.

A: Have we met before?

B: Have we? I don't know.

A: I think we have.

B: When?

A: I don't know.

B: No.

In this case the 'wants' stay the same for both characters, so there's no change in unit.

Don't take my word for it – have a go.

Actions

What do you do if you really want something, but you can't seem to get it? The answer, of course, other than give up, is that you change the way you go about *trying to get* what you want. You take action. In the language of acting, you employ **Actions**. A good word to use here is tactics. You use tactics to help you get what you want. Literally, you try a range of different approaches – or Actions – to help you reach your goal.

For an actor working on a script, the question to ask then is this: 'What different, observable practical Actions could my character use in order to achieve each Objective and overcome any Barriers?' The crucial word in that sentence is 'observable'. Each varying Action you use – each tactic you employ – needs to be noticeable to every audience member. And since traditional theatre is a medium presented entirely, as it were, in long-shot, you will need some skill to communicate each of these Actions to your audience.

Here's a description of a provocative exercise I used recently to help student actors understand Actions and to highlight the need to make Actions observable. First, I sat on a chair in the rehearsal room. Next, I provoked my students with the idea that, though I had possession of the chair, they urgently wanted to take it from me. This of course is a 'What If?' with an overtly built-in Objective. I was challenging my students to use their imagination to motivate their desire for the chair.

How do you get someone to give up their chair? It helps, of course, if the rules are on your side. If you're on a busy train and someone has taken your reserved seat, you might try politely showing them your ticket reservation. If this doesn't work, you could track down the train guard and get official help. What though if you don't have a reservation? Maybe you have some implied form of Agreed Power: perhaps you are elderly or pregnant or disabled, and the person already seated is feeling kind. But what if you're not or they're not?

Back to me, sat on a chair in the rehearsal room. The first time I tried this exercise with a group of student actors, I stated simply: 'I have this chair. You want it. Try to get it from me.' This first group – wary perhaps of directly crossing invisible barriers – tried to involve me in a range of imaginary scenarios. 'My (invisible) grandad is very ill and he needs to sit down.' 'This other (identical) chair here is much nicer – it's padded.' 'The floor is melting!' (It wasn't.) It was easy for me to dismiss their attempts at persuasion because – another key word here – there was very little genuinely at *stake* for me. The students were simply play-acting and I was (rather meanly) refusing to engage with their imagined scenarios.

After explaining this to the group, I invited them to try again. This time I'd barely finished speaking the challenge before I found myself standing, chairless. Two students had gone for Route One – stomping over and yanking the chair from underneath me.

In the next session I offered the following adjustment: 'I have this chair. You want it. Try to get it from me without touching me or the chair.' What I was doing, of course, was imposing both an Objective ('You want this chair') and a Barrier ('You can't use physical force'). Yet thirty seconds later I was again chairless – two students standing very close by had screamed in unison until I had no choice but to flee. What was going on here? I think it's important to relate Actions to Power (see p. 39). I suppose my own style of teaching had granted the students implicit permission to be direct – aggressive even – within an acting exercise. They held implied Agreed Power.

I needed to learn fast. My hearing depended on it. In the next session I told the group, 'I have this chair. You want it. Try to get it from me without touching me or the chair, and without harming me physically in any way – for example, without harming my five senses.' Their response? A pause. Then one student carrying an unopened bottle of drinking water marched over and threatened to drip water onto my head unless I moved. Other group members voiced their disapproval at the plan. I stayed sitting – and got wet.

Then things began to get more complex. There was a secretive tactical discussion during which they began to plan more sophisticated, more psychological actions – including more gently persuasive methods – that might separate me from my chair. I was offered a bribe – a rather tasty-looking cupcake. Heroically, I refused.

The group's default reaction was aggression but, this time, psychological aggression. One student snatched my glasses and fled the room, calling out that she would only return them if I yielded the chair. She returned empty-handed and I didn't move. A further quick secret discussion and then the students announced a mass walk-out: 'We're all leaving right now and we'll stay gone and you'll be fired'. Amazingly, they left. I held my ground (and the chair – rather tightly). Five minutes later they returned. More discussion. Several seemed to give up, forming a circle. 'This has got really boring. We're just going to sit over here and talk until you give in.'

A few minutes on, feeling ignored and a bit boring, I gave in, stood up, and began to walk towards the group. There was an instant stampede, a scuffle, and a single triumphant winner.

By the end of the exercise my students had put into practice the tactical use of Actions to help them achieve an Objective. It felt like something of a breakthrough. Acting teachers traditionally sit on the edge of practical work – directing, commenting, criticising. I had crossed an invisible line and been on the receiving end of quite a range of skilful tactical manipulation. Something else: I had experienced a realisation that Power, both real and perceived, really is a key factor in guiding the tactics people use when they choose an Action. One of the most challenging Psychological Barriers to achieving your Objective will always be the threat posed to you by the other person's Power, whether it be Agreed, Abuse, Reward, Knowledge, Connection or Personal.

There are potential problems when exploring Actions within a script rehearsal. Actors can obsess over finding the right word to express what they are doing – a distraction that can ironically turn focus away from their partner. Also, the indiscriminate playing of Actions risks distorting the play. Here's why. If your character wants a chair – or a room, or a kiss, or anything else another character has the power to withhold – there's a huge range of types of Action that you can employ to achieve your Objective, ranging from gently persuasive to heavily aggressive, with lots of levels in between. Any actor working on a playscript must stick to the text and in particular to the words spoken by the character. Yet it's highly unlikely that those words will fit with a delivery that is both gently persuasive and also heavily aggressive. The playwright has already visualised the scene in their head and hopes you will adopt tactics that roughly match that vision.

Another problem is one of language. What's the difference between an Action and an Objective? Hopefully the section above will have led you to know this difference; but some of the literature out there on Actions can be confusing.

Also, what's the difference between an Action and an Activity? One highly valuable, but sometimes (in my view) overused exercise in actor training is a variation on Stanislavski's **solitude in public** work. This typically asks the actor to forensically recreate a private space at home – a bedroom, say – using bedding, personal possessions and so on. There are at least three key questions underlying such work: Can the actor commit to a sense of being in private while being observed? Can the actor re-imagine in forensic detail the Given Circumstances that are now being revisited? And can the actor remain interesting to watch even when working privately and without a script? For me, it all depends on the actor's understanding of the difference between an Objective and an Action, and between an Action and an Activity.

Here's a brief mini case-study that applies right now. I need to take a break from writing this because I'm rehearsing later, but first my dog needs a walk. My Objective right now is *I want to clarify to you the difference between an Action and an Activity*. There's a big physical barrier – *you and I are not in the same room* – but there's also a psychological one – *my dog needs a walk*. The dog-walk is an activity that needs to happen, but it doesn't concern you, and it shouldn't really impact on you. Even so it's making me a little edgy because at this point in my writing there's an important point to clarify. But I'm also amused because my dog is now staring bleakly at me as if he fears he might not actually get his walk. Actually, there's now a new barrier too – *he's started whining in a quiet way that sounds a bit like fingernails on a blackboard.* So time to prepare things for the walk.

Where was I? When is something an Action and when is it simply an Activity? It's easiest to tell the difference, I believe, when there are two people involved. An Activity can be performed near someone else without really affecting them (ironing clothes, reading emails, getting dressed, even perhaps sleeping). Whereas an Action that is energised by an Objective – especially a high-stakes Objective where you've a lot to lose – is something that should always be felt and received by the other person. If you want my chair, you may taunt me and I will feel taunted; you may tempt me and I will feel tempted.

An Action provokes then the need for a *re*action. Of course if you're being provoked, you may choose not to react. In reality you are choosing to hide your reaction. At the very least you are trying to ignore the Action. You try to tempt me from my chair with the promise of a tasty cupcake; I pretend I don't fancy it and offer you a defiant smile. I keep the seat; you keep the cake, and a palpable feeling of conflict remains. Physically, very little happens; yet there's a strong sense that something is at stake. And anyone watching closely (which is of course what theatre and film audiences do) will have observed both an act of temptation and the effortful resisting of temptation. It's at least interesting – not least because it's like real life.

Here's one way to visualise you character's need to combine an Objective with a suitable Action (or a range of Actions). Both those terms, Objective and Action, suggest some sort of active focusing of energy towards another person. What if your energy was light? What if your whole body was covered with points of light? (I'm imagining one of those curious motion capture suits dotted with lights.) What if you had one hundred swivel-headed lamps lightly resting on the surface of your body and they could float away from you like heated atoms?

The simple idea is the more keenly you want something from someone, the more your little lamps turn towards that person and illuminate them. And the more aggressively you take action to achieve your want – in other words, the stronger the Action – the more your lamps drift across and place themselves on that other person. You can imagine that at moments of a character's most extreme crisis (battling to save a relationship or even a life), all one hundred lamps have left you and are clinging to the other character. What if the stake is lower? What if you risk less? Then only some of your lamps illuminate that other person and fewer of them make the journey through space towards the other person.

The potential value of such a visualisation is this. There's a marked difference between simply shining a light on something from a distance and actually 'risking' some of those lights by sending them away from you. Literally, it requires you to commit some energy and diminish your own. You become less distinct and perhaps more vulnerable.

I suppose my atom-lamps visualisation is a distant cousin of Stanislavski's **circles of attention**. The aim is, to some extent, the same – to help you, the actor, be clear about where you most of all need to place your mental focus.

We're getting pretty forensic, of course, in this discussion of the dynamics between people. From an acting point of view, there's a lot going on high above this business of Actions, and reactions to Actions. The playwright has provided you and your fellow actors with a scenario – a 'What If?' – along with associated Given Circumstances. You have inherited a cast of characters who have been given words to speak. There are a few stage directions. The director and actors have taken over from there. You have created a detailed profile of your character, drawing on the play and on your research into the context of the play. You have worked with others to identify Units, making a full script easier to digest, and within each Unit you have identified for your character an Objective with corresponding possible Physical and Psychological Barriers. That's your map – your planning. Now, in the liveness of rehearsal, you can employ one or more Actions to help you achieve your Objective. Now, your fellow actor – fully planned, like you – is ready to trade tactics. And it's this last bit, I would suggest – the tactical use of Actions – that needs to remain flexible, strategic, ever-changing, and private. Achieve that, and you'll create something immediate, authentic, psychologically real, that looks and feels subtly different and fresh during every performance.

Tool No. 19: Imagining Sensations

The five senses (sight, hearing, touch, taste and smell) are, of course, not the same as the emotions. They are linked in that an intense sensory experience may well stimulate a strong emotional response. For example, sudden pain can cause fear or anger. But mild background sensory stimulation is around us all the time and much of it remains just that – background. As I write this, if I listen, I can hear a cartoon showing on the television in another room, a song playing on the radio in the kitchen, a jet plane flying overhead, and my neighbour mowing her lawn. I'm looking at my computer screen and keyboard in turn, but my peripheral vision tells me that my dog is lying in the hallway, sleeping soundly. I've just enjoyed a shortbread biscuit and I'm about to take a sip of tea. The keyboard sits on a cold metal pull-out drawer which I rest my hands on between typing. When I'm thinking I stroke my chin, which is unshaven. The dog has just rolled onto his back into a funny position which makes him look like he's just fallen off the ceiling. My senses are being bombarded with background stimulation, but none of it is enough to make me break off writing. I've just saved progress on my computer and the program I'm using has answered my command to 'Save' with a chirpy note – 'bling!' – which sounds like some sort of flourish. Now I think about it, that 'bling!' is an important part of the writing process. It tells me I'm making progress and so encourages me to write a bit more. Put simply, the effect is as follows:

Sensory stimulus (*causes an*) emotional reaction (*which encourages*) action

'Bling!'   I'm pleased with progress   write a bit more

The point though is this: while an actor's awareness of their five senses is important, you mustn't let your sensory awareness dominate when it's not of real significance to the story you're helping to tell. Look again at the (real) scene I've just described as I sat typing. If this was a scene in a film, what aspects of the scene would be most important for the audience? Of course, it depends on the story and on the character. If the character is a writer who cannot tear themselves away from their writing, then the presence of an ignored dog who is getting restless tells you something about the writer's state of mind. If the character is a spy who is accessing someone else's computer, then the chin-stroking might be helpful in revealing the pressure on him. Some of the other sensory details – the biscuit, the lawnmower, the cold metal, even in this case the dog – are probably irrelevant distractions to both actor and audience. Of course on a film set you are already coping with a range of pressures – not the least of which is the presence of a great gang of crew members, watching only to see that their bit of the process is working well. You're worrying about continuity, trying to remember lines, limiting your movement so that you don't cast a shadow on your fellow actor, trying to fight for your 'want' despite the (in character) barriers that block your way. If you don't notice the lawnmower supposedly buzzing away in the background, whisper it, but no-one will notice or even care.

You're an actor, not a member of the X-Men. Your most impressive powers are that you imagine things in a way that other people find accessible. I like that mnemonic KISS – Keep It Simple, Stupid. Don't let yourself (or other people) clog up your creative faculty – your ability to transmit what you imagine. You can't, for example, play two objectives – two 'wants' – simultaneously. (If you're stuck choosing between two, one of them is almost certainly a barrier). You can't either transmit everything that is happening to your senses when in character; or rather it doesn't help if you strain to do so. Prioritise. If the sensory stimulus is essentially background – leave it there. If it's very much relevant to the story – and especially if the sensory stimulus prompts an emotion which prompts a desire for action ('bling!') – then imagine it, and imagine it hard.

How hard do you have to work to imagine such sensory stimuli? To some extent actors in the twenty-first century are spoiled compared to those of a hundred or more years ago. In the late nineteenth century the playwright August Strindberg wrote how he longed for a theatre in which the set for a kitchen might consist of more than just 'painted pots and pans' lit by distorting footlights. The quick march towards the naturalism Strindberg sought has now left us with a theatre, and of course a world of film and television, in which actors are surrounded by sets, costumes, hairstyles etc that are acutely realistic. To a high degree you can just open up your senses to the sights, sounds and textures that the designers and crew have created for you.

When is this not the case? Interestingly, those worlds in which transformational character acting is still valued also tend to be the areas in which the actor must make the effort to imagine and project sensory stimulation. The small-cast plays of Steven Berkoff and John Godber, for example, often require the actors to energetically evoke a world of sights, sounds, textures, tastes and smells. Radio drama relies heavily on the actors allowing their voices to be infused with imagined images, tastes, smells. And the language of William Shakespeare is painstakingly designed to fill the heads of audiences with sensory stimuli whether it be Caliban's 'thousand twangling instruments', which hum about his ears, or any one of the myriad images which flash shape, colour and emotion into the listener's mind.

So how can you develop your ability to imagine sensory stimuli? As part of the process of training to be an actor, quite a lot of time should be spent on improvisations that stimulate your five senses. When I was at drama school we did a lot of this. We'd be survivors of a plane crash in the desert, suffering pain from our injuries, intense heat from the wind and sun, thirst from lack of water. Or we'd be homeless people settling down to sleep in a city square, suffering hunger from lack of food, cold from the snow and wind and we'd huddle together for warmth. Or we'd be aliens dropped in from another galaxy, armed perhaps with no sight, but with a really good sense of hearing. Each actor/alien would discover a unique way of moving as the task of sensorally scanning and recording this new environment began. Or we'd be animals caged in a zoo, left for the night to hear and smell the threats and temptations which came on the air to our ears and our noses.

Such improvisations are invaluable in keeping your imagination well-exercised. They should take place behind closed doors with no formal audience. They should be open-ended so that no story and no result is demanded of you. The purpose is simply to practise imagining things which stimulate your senses. They're great fun – serious and valuable, but also playful and childlike.

Just as important are solo sensory exercises, ideally watched by your fellow acting students. You might imagine being somewhere alone having to cope with a range of real, imagined or recalled sensory stimuli. The aim is to achieve something of Stanislavski's state of public solitude – being as focused as possible on the things within the imagined world, while remaining relatively uninfluenced by observers.

The athlete's journey towards peak fitness encompasses much more than daily workouts at the gym. Likewise, the actor needs to, as it were, stretch imagination muscles all the time through spontaneous 'what if?' games. What if you suddenly smell a terrible odour? What if someone really attractive smiles at you? What if you unexpectedly hear a song on the radio that reminds you of a special memory? What if, when you're feeling low, a friend arrives and wraps their arms around you?

Example: Natasha from *Three Sisters*

Read and rehearse this short scene below from Act Four. There's an undercurrent of loss as we distantly hear soldiers (for so long the lifeblood of the place) leaving the town. Also, some distance away, an unseen duel is scheduled between the Baron Tuzenbach and Soleni, which could prove fatal (we don't yet know that it will). There's a spectrum of sensory stimuli to be imagined and explored – live sights (e.g. Natasha appearing at a window above, the children, the newspaper) and live sounds (e.g. distant marching, birds, crying, music playing), plus remembered sensations (such as tastes and smells and extreme cold). Take time and trouble to revisit your own memories of the same or of similar experiences and sensations. When you've arrived at a focused state of mind – one in which these experiences and sensory stimuli are available to your imagination – you're ready to begin the scene.

ANDREI
> The present is terrible, but when I think of the future, the present seems good! I feel so light, so free; there is a light in the distance, I see freedom. I see myself and my children freeing ourselves from vanities, from kvass, from goose baked with cabbage, from after-dinner naps, from base idleness ...

FERAPON
> He says two thousand people froze to death. Everyone was terrified, apparently. In Petersburg or Moscow, I can't remember which.

ANDREI *[Overcome by a tender emotion]*
> My dear sisters, my beautiful sisters! *[Crying]* Masha, my sister ...

NATASHA *[At the window]*
> Who's being so loud out here? Is that you, Andrei? You'll wake little Sophie. – Il ne faut pas faire du bruit, la Sophie

est dormée deja. Vous êtes un ours. – *[Angrily]* If you want to talk, then give the pram and the baby to somebody else. Ferapont, take the pram!

FERAPONT
Yes ma'am. *[Takes the pram.]*

ANDREI *[Confused]*
I was speaking quietly.

NATASHA *[At the window, nursing her boy]*
Bobik! Naughty Bobik! Bad little Bobik!

ANDREI *[Looking through the papers]*
All right, I'll look them over and sign if necessary, and you can take them back to the offices …

[Goes into house reading papers; FERAPONT takes the pram to the back of the garden.]

NATASHA *[At the window]*
Bobik, what's your mother's name? There we are! And who's this? That's Auntie Olga. Say, 'Hello, Auntie Olga!'

[Two wandering musicians are playing on a violin and a harp. VERSHININ, OLGA, and ANFISA come out of the house and listen for a minute in silence.]

Tool No. 20: Generating Emotion

I know – emotion is not something you can just generate, like electricity. And frankly actors are set up to fail in this area so long as directors or acting teachers or audience members demand that you should be able to burst into tears on cue, like some performing sideshow attraction. (You might know the witty lyric from the musical *A Chorus Line* in which beleaguered student actor Diana Morales lists wild imaginary journeys in which, at every turn 'I felt nothing!')

In truth it's best not to strain and stretch to feel emotion. Instead, try sticking with the 'uniting' method explored earlier in this Section. Work out a route through the story by identifying what it is, at each point, that your character is fighting for (your Objective) and what gets in the way (the Barriers). Then identify possible Actions. Then plough your energies into imagining things that are most relevant and strive for real moment-by-moment interaction with your fellow actor(s). You should become drawn into each moment of the story and, at each point, when the conditions in the rehearsal room are right, genuine, spontaneous emotion should emerge and it may take you by surprise. What if you don't ever manage to generate emotion? Well, if you've read this book from the start and performed the exercises, you will now also be armed with a sophisticated practical knowledge of human non-verbal and verbal communication, much of which results from experiencing (or trying to hide) emotion. This stuff is invaluable in rehearsal when you're exploring relationships and developing your character. But it can also rescue you in performance. Your knowledge is an aspect of your technique – something to fall back on. And the chances are that if you find yourself onstage without any true sense of emotion ('I feel nothing!') then you can use your knowledge to help you. Just consciously take on, for example, the appropriate tension, eye contact and pace of speech, and – astonishingly enough – your mind will feel something going on and start to connect you to a spontaneous emotional state. And if it doesn't, it's unlikely anyone will notice because the behavioural side of your performance (the part that audiences can observe) looks right. Think of your knowledge as your emergency jump-leads – carry a set with you at all times.

Stanislavski recognised that emotions are difficult to lasso and harness, especially when a role has been performed repeatedly for some months. As an actor he had a bit of a crisis of confidence at one point and decided that the goal and the way forward was to feel real emotion at all times. Psychiatry and psychoanalysis were growing fast at this point; the concept of the 'subconscious' was becoming an accepted scientific truism. Stanislavski pondered how the emotions seemed somehow to be anchored in our subconscious selves. His ever-evolving System started to focus more and more on using 'conscious means [to] reach the subconscious'. He started experimenting with **emotion memory**.

Essentially, an emotion memory exercise challenges you, the actor, to revisit emotional experiences so that an intense memory-related emotion resurfaces. Since this is also something patients do in psychotherapy, you may have spotted a danger here. In therapeutic situations, patients' psychological state is paramount and all work takes place in a safe and confidential environment.

Actors, as we know, are all mad. Yet despite this, those untrained in working with traumatised people are allowed to tear actors' innermost traumas from their scarred subconsciousness before placing such excavation on public view. And more often than not the actors thank them for it. (Final proof of madness, you might say.)

Actually, emotion memory exercises are undoubtedly valuable in that they stretch you as an actor. It's usually a pleasant shock for an actor to experience, in a workshop situation, the spontaneous arrival of an intense emotion, especially if the emotion is one which they secretly struggle to generate.

Even so, as an acting teacher I find I can be uncomfortable in my position as midwife to the revisiting of intense emotional memories. I don't want to leave anyone feeling depressed and saddened as they sit in their bedroom later that night, long-buried traumas swirling around them. So I always set a few ground rules which help to reduce anxiety and keep our status as equal as possible.

Firstly, you, the actor, get to choose the memory. Secondly, you decide whether real names are used. Thirdly, either of us can end the activity as and when we think it necessary. Fourthly, the other student actors get to watch (acting is a public activity). And lastly, everyone has to agree that what is revealed during the workshop remains strictly confidential. I find that if such a workshop is explained, carefully managed, allowed its own pace, and the five rules are strictly adhered to, then the outcome is successful for all. Acting students become more able to emote spontaneously and to do so in front of others, and there's a greater sense of trust between us all.

As ever, though, there are doubts as to the value and necessity of emotion memory exercises. Stanislavski was caught out when one of his own actors became highly emotional when recalling the funeral of his recently deceased father. Deeply moved, Stanislavski comforted the performer, only to learn later that the actor's father was still very much alive. (The actor had used his imagination.) Interestingly, that actor, Michael Chekhov, later became something of an acting guru in the United States. He's probably best-known for the technique of the **psychological gesture**, whereby a person's psychological state is given expression through a seemingly unconscious physical gesture.

Example: Natasha from *Three Sisters*

Read and rehearse the short section of scene below from Act Four. In this final sequence at the end of the play there's a sense that Natasha is now in full control, confidently appointing her lover, Protopopov, as well as her husband, Andrei, to babysitting duty, planning bold changes to the garden, and, in a neat reversal, daring to criticise Irina's dress sense. It's been a long journey for Natasha and we hear her in full stream of conciousness mode as she speaks aloud her plans. What though are the other characters thinking, but not saying?

As you plan for rehearsal, use the full range of techniques described above – identifying Units, clarifying Objectives, establishing Physical and Psychological Barriers, trying out different Actions – and also hunt for moments from your own experience that chime emotionally. Be imaginative in seeking experiences from your own life that you could draw on. Have you, for instance, ever got your own back on a bully? How did you feel about it afterwards? A word or two of warning. You'll need to match Anton Chekhov's understanding of the mind to work out what's really going on in this tiny sequence. Chekhov is after all the master of subtext so his characters often seem to be saying one thing while thinking something else (perhaps related, but different). Remember too that in real life people don't plan monologues – they become so because other people decide not to speak. Make sure you link your ideas back to Natasha's prior experiences. Refer for one last time to her Character Profile Sheet in the Appendix.

When you think you're ready, set to work, using all the force of your imagination.

[Enter NATASHA.]

NATASHA. *[To the maid]*
What? Protopopov will sit with little Sophie, and Andrei can take little Bobik out. Children are such a bother ... *[To IRINA]* Irina, you're going tomorrow – such a shame. Do stay on just one more week. *[Sees KULIGIN and screams; he laughs and takes off his false beard and whiskers]* You really frightened me! *[To IRINA]* I'm so used to having you around – do you think it will be easy for me, seeing you go? I'm going to put Andrei and his violin in your room – let him fiddle away in there! – and we'll put little Sophie in Andrei's room. Such a sweet, beautiful, child! What a little darling! Today she looked at me with such pretty eyes and said 'Mamma!'

KULIGIN
She's a beautiful child, it's true.

NATASHA
So I shall have the place to myself tomorrow. *[Sighs]* First I'm going to cut down that avenue of fir-trees, then the maple here. It's so ugly at nights ... *[To IRINA]* That belt doesn't suit

you at all, dear ... It's in poor taste. And I'll have lots and lots
of little flowers planted here, and they'll smell so – *[Severely]*
Why is there a fork lying here on the seat? *[Going towards the
house, to the maid]* I said, why is there a fork lying here on the
seat? *[Shouts]* Don't answer me back!

KULIGIN

Temper, temper! *[A march is played off; they all listen.]*

OLGA

They're leaving.

END

When then should you use emotion memory to help your acting?
I'd suggest sparingly, when you are struggling to reach the level
of emotional depth you strongly suspect lies within a scene. It's
very possible to skim along the surface of a play in rehearsal,
resisting the urge to dive below and explore the emotional deeps.
After all, open displays of emotion can seem embarrassing, even
in the rehearsal room. Part of your job as an actor, however, is to
sidestep such embarrassment and just go for it. But how? Sitting
in a circle remembering your own personal emotional lows or
highs is surely very different from standing on a stage trying to
project real emotion while in character.

At its simplest there are two routes. You could try bringing all
your imaginative powers to bear on the combined stimuli of the
given circumstances, the 'want' you're fighting for, and the
barriers which block the way. Or you could find an emotionally
charged situation in your own past which closely resembles the
one your character currently finds themselves in, and then let
your mind blend the two together into a single experience. This
approach, which is usually referred to as **substitution**, can work
really well, mainly because your audience can't read your mind
so they're happy to believe that your emotions belong to the
character rather than to you.

As with any attempt to generate real emotion, there are pitfalls. As an actor rehearsing or performing a play, you run the risk of starting to feel inadequate as, at each running of the unit, the repetition of the substituted memory starts to lose its intensity. Such fading is not only inevitable but also necessary – partly, it's how we cope with grief in real life. You could try switching memories, finding something else that upsets you (if that's the emotion you're seeking). But how much fun is that? And what can it lead to? I once heard of an actor performing in a long run of a Shakespearean tragedy who became so unhappy at losing the effects of his own sad memories that he started buying butterflies – which only live for one day – so that he could mourn each of their deaths nightly onstage. One day a Large Cabbage White failed to die on the appointed day and the actor, desperate for an experience to use, killed his own mother with a fencing foil.

Of course the story above is entirely made-up and utter nonsense (how many actors can afford to buy a butterfly every day?), but if you even for a moment began to believe the tale, then maybe that says more about the actor's dilemma than it does about your gullibility...

One way to explore further different styles of acting is to consider different types of theatre space. Central to the skill of acting and reacting is an actor's use of space. There are lots of different theatre spaces: proscenium, theatre-in-the-round, endstage, thrust, traverse (aka transverse, alley or corridor), promenade – all of which can be created in non-traditional theatre spaces. Since this is a book about acting, I'm going to skip (with apologies) much of the detail on each of the various types of staging. What I will say here though is that endstage, thrust and traverse staging formats each represent something of a mix between proscenium and in-the-round – two key styles that we will soon consider in more detail.

Size matters

Whatever the space you are acting in, you must always know how big your acting should be. Of course the defining factor in determining how big you need to be, is the play itself.

Some plays demand that the actors turn up or turn down the size of their performance throughout the script. I think of these as breakout texts – you may be striving for a sense of naturalism one minute, but turn the page and you are expected to leap into a cartoonish stereotype. The earlier plays by John Godber exemplify this: the popular piece *Bouncers* ranges from rap-style rhyming text to confessional monologue to Pythonesque comic satire, and settles on various points in between. An actor working on an early Godber play needs, therefore, to be a skilled

Inhabiter, Storyteller and Classicist (see p. xv). They must be able to variously live the role, show a huge caricature to the audience and rap to a beat. It can get confusing.

I recently started experimenting with a sort of projection dial – a simple way of thinking that allows actors to identify one of four different levels of performance. The idea is that we agree in rehearsal which of the four settings is appropriate for a specific section of text. Each setting has in common the letters AB; so I call it the 'ABility scale'. The four levels are:

- LABoratory
- HABitat
- TABleaux
- CABaret

The four terms should suggest to you the four different levels:

1 **Laboratory acting** is close-up acting that is forensically real – for example, in a filmed drama.
2 **Habitat acting** is a little more projected. Typically you will still be performing realistically and apparently unselfconsciously (rather like TV's earliest *Big Brother* contestants who became used to the hidden cameras), but you will be using some technique and awareness to reach your audience with aspects of voice and movement. This is the sort of acting required when you're in a naturalistic play produced in a studio theatre.
3 **Tableaux acting** acknowledges the theatricality of theatre. Character and relationships are expressed through selected images, larger than life, that may echo the visual simplicity and power of dramatic public sculpture (such as those memorials that feature character archetypes – the Brave Soldier, the Protective Mother, and so on).
4 **Cabaret acting** celebrates (or mocks) via the cartoonish stereotype, using big energy to propel your huge performance to a far-off back row.

There's a clear relationship between my ABility scale and Inhabiting/Storytelling – the two most common modes of performance. Laboratory and Habitat performance work (Levels 1 and 2) typically requires internalised, psychologically-driven Inhabiter acting while Tableaux and Cabaret acting (Levels 3 and 4) typically requires externalised, image-rich Storyteller acting. The challenge for you as an actor is to identify (ideally, working with a smart director alongside you) which of the four approaches each section of the current play demands from you. If you discover that at some point the text demands non-naturalistic, image-rich acting, you're going to have to commit to delivering this at Level 3 or Level 4 – and you'll have to let go of some of your more forensic Inhabiter truthfulness. I actually think this is a crucial point for actors, including those trained at conservatoire schools where forensic realism can be all. My first professional directing work required me to direct actors only at Level 3 (Tableaux) and Level 4 (Cabaret). We were delivering street theatre-style performances of issue-based work to large groups of teenagers; high energy and big comedy was key. One or two cast members who were recent conservatoire graduates struggled initially to step up to the required higher performance size. There are lessons here, too, for actors who have sidestepped drama school training. A lengthy spell as a star amateur actor may have been built on skilful Storyteller acting. If so, you'll have to work hard to let go of this when you appear alongside professionals in your first naturalistic production.

Proscenium v round: a comparison

In the West, **proscenium theatre** is the type found most often inside older theatre buildings. Based loosely on a classical model, but growing directly out of the Italian Renaissance, proscenium theatres present a simple picture frame to an audience. The actors and the audience are in effect in separate, interconnected rooms, though the actors are on a raised stage several feet above the front row. The stage side of a proscenium theatre is typically something of a box of tricks – scenery and props can be flown in using the flying equipment and tower, there may well be trapdoors, tricks can be played with the backdrop, such as the false rear wall used in the stage thriller *Woman In Black*.

Even though proscenium theatres are pretty well everywhere, it doesn't actually follow that they provide the best or easiest theatre shape for performance. All audience members are facing roughly the same way so the actors have to frequently turn their performances outwards in one broad direction. The actors also need to work hard (with a director sitting out in the auditorium during rehearsals) to avoid too much interrupting of audience sightlines. And the people seated on one level can't see the people sat at the other levels, so the audience is less of a community than it might be in other spaces. In fact proscenium theatres with split-level seating have been criticised for being socially divisive. Typically, the lower stalls seating area closest to the stage has the best view, therefore the most expensive seats; the circle above has the next-best view – though you can find yourself looking quite steeply down at the actors; and, beyond that, the upper circle and the balcony (also known as the gods or the 'nosebleed section') found in many proscenium theatres have the worst view, and so the cheapest seats. It follows that someone watching a play from the upper reaches of a theatre will have a quite different experience of a performance from someone seated centrally in the stalls. Indeed it's easy to feel ignored up there by actors whose necks (and sometimes vocal cords) seems only to stretch so far.

In contrast to all this, a **theatre-in-the-round** space usually stages theatre on a round stage. In fact in some spaces theatre-in-the-round might be better-named 'theatre-in-the-square'. In these instances, there's a central square-shaped space with seating butting against each of the four edges of the stage. But whatever the shape of the theatre-in-the-round stage – round, square or rectangular – the audience sits facing both the stage and (beyond the stage) a block of other audience-members. Theatre-in-the-round has been described as a communal experience since you can see other people reacting to the actors. You are also unlikely to ever be in a bad seat distant from the action since, with the audience on all four sides, a large number of seats can be fitted in quite close to the stage.

As regards acting styles, to generalise, a proscenium theatre tends to function best when hosting a play that needs Storyteller acting while a theatre-in-the-round tends to work best when hosting a play that needs Inhabiter acting. This is to do with focus. A play that needs Storyteller acting requires its actors to directly address the whole audience in one go while a play that needs Inhabiter acting requires its actors to work together to build an authentic-seeming world that the surrounding audience can believe in, while remaining on the outside. If you're ever in the small English town of Scarborough you'll find a highly inti-mate theatre-in-the-round (strictly-speaking, a theatre-in-the-*square*) seating 406 people in a single space; a large proscenium theatre seating well over two thousand people in stalls, a circle and seven boxes; and, curiously, Europe's biggest open-air theatre, set out in a kind of endstage format, with seating for around six thousand. Alan Ayckbourn's round theatre of choice takes its name from his former mentor, Stephen Joseph. Joseph was a theatre entrepreneur and provocateur who achieved some surprising things during his short career as a professional theatre director and manager. I mention him here because, among his many achievements, he was an expert in theatre-in-the-round. He observed it in action in professional theatres in the USA – including in Dallas and in Washington, DC – and subsequently launched it professionally in the UK in 1955. One of Stephen Joseph's immediate challenges in 1955 was to help actors and directors discover the difference between acting on a proscenium stage and acting on a round theatre stage. He labelled the typical proscenium actor's approach **linear projection** – the ability to push your performance and characterisation outwards towards a horizontally divided audience that is partly below you, and also partly high above you. The term captures quite well, I think, the somewhat mono-directional actor-to-audience dynamic typically seen in proscenium theatres. He labelled round theatre acting **organic projection**. This title reflects, Joseph wrote, 'an acceptance by actors that they are three-dimensional figures, occupying three-dimensional space'.

Acting on the proscenium stage

A pure proscenium theatre stages its drama entirely inside the arch – as it were, entirely in the other room. This means that proscenium actors need to be continually aware of where they are in relation to an audience that is spread around the auditorium, in the much larger room located beyond the arch.

I'm going to assume here that you've had some experience of performing in a proscenium-style space – perhaps long ago in the school Nativity play or perhaps as a public speaker addressing a group sitting, or standing, solely on one side of you. You'll know that the larger the group, the wider and stronger your span of linear projection (using both voice and gesture) will need to be. If you've ever spoken in public and had to cope with an interrupted view of part of your audience (because of a pillar, a lectern, etc) then you will, too, already have an instinct for the problem of masking – when one actor prevents the audience from seeing another actor by standing in the way. Whatever choices you make to improve communication in a proscenium theatre, it's clear that the unnaturalness of the situation demands a considered response – technique in other words. Partly, the essence of proscenium acting technique is contained within that term linear projection.

In a large theatre, linear projection is hard enough for the solo performer to achieve. As soon as you bring on a second performer, things complicate considerably. A proscenium stage peppered with actors quickly becomes, for the director, something of an exercise in crowd control. One of the most common problems in ensemble proscenium acting occurs when you, the actor, located downstage (i.e. closer to the audience) need to interact with a second actor located further upstage. What to do? Turn and face the other actor, offering your back to the audience? Face the audience, but talk to the other actor anyway, even though you're not looking at them? Walk upstage so that you are parallel with the other actor, then turn to them as you speak? ('Right Ear Acting', my old acting tutor called this.) It's tempting for a director working in rehearsal to solve these emerging crowd control problems as they occur: as empty onstage spaces fill up, new ones must be found. Of course, the space between characters must reflect the psychological relationship between characters, but, on a proscenium stage, masking can become the dominant problem. Panicked or first-time directors working with a large cast will quickly fall back on the chorus line: audiences are presented with actors lined up across an upstage section of stage – spectators in effect – who basically watch, while the more important characters move freely around in the remaining stage space.

Proscenium theatre directors still sometimes incorporate what some older actors refer to as 'meeting your audience'. Here, a lead actor is moved downstage, Storyteller-style, to connect with the whole of the (horizontally divided) audience. This can be powerful – it's an essential part of pantomime for instance. But it can be problematical within a naturalistic drama since, for the characters in the play, the audience must always remain invisible beyond the fourth wall. A determined director will need to impose a character motivation to justify such a downstage move: a downstage window, mirror or similar fourth-wall feature can help here.

If this all sounds rather technical – artificial even – it is. Indeed, if you act on a proscenium stage you are always at least dimly aware of your status as a theatre technician. You can often glimpse, with your peripheral vision, the unseen (to an audience) workings as offstage actors wait their turn and crew members keep the machine of the production moving. You may too be very aware of the stage lighting, which can be very bright since some of your audience members are far away (you may have to train yourself not to squint in the light). The brightness of the stage lamps can also make the auditorium virtually disappear – it may take effort to remember to reach those unseen faraway audience members. Also, if you're acting in a comic play in a large theatre, audience laughter can come at you in waves – meaning that you'll need to make moment-by-moment adjustment to the pausing within your speech. All in all, you get a strong sense in proscenium theatre of an illusory world that can be very distracting. This can affect actors on at least two levels: the Inhabiter actor risks being continually jolted out of their imagined reality by offstage activity and technical needs, including the need to sustain linear projection, while the Storyteller actor risks being continually seduced towards the darkened breathing auditorium and away from fellow actors. There's more: in the words of Ben Kingsley – who, unusually, learned to act in the round before mastering proscenium theatre acting technique – you need to beware of the 'ghastly tricks' of more experienced proscenium actors 'like trying to upstage your fellow actor or fiddling around with a prop to get the audience's attention'.

It's plain, though, that proscenium theatre encourages actors to reach through the fourth wall and engage with the audience. Indeed, traditional pantomime relies on the playfulness that is part of this dynamic. Here's a moment from *Edward Gant's Amazing Feats of Loneliness* by Anthony Neilson, which draws on some of the conventions of pantomime:

LUDD
That is a strangely depressing story.

Pause

BEAR ONE
May I have my tea and cake now?

Pause

LUDD
Yes. Of course.

BEAR TWO
Is that imaginary tea you're having?

LUDD

No, sod this – I'm not having this! This is ludicrous! GANT?!

He turns to the audience

I'm sorry, ladies and gentlemen, but I can't go on with this.
I'M NOT GOING ON WITH THIS, GANT, DO YOU HEAR ME?!

BEAR TWO *(whispers)*
What are you doing, Ludd?!

LUDD

I'm stopping the show, Jasper – that's all right, isn't it? To
just stop the show when you feel like it?!

BEAR TWO *(whispers)*
Of course it's not all right!

LUDD

Well it's all right for Gant – it's all right for him, isn't it? So
why's it not all right for me?! COME ON, GANT! SHOW
YOURSELF!

Bear Two attempts to manhandle him off the stage.

LUDD

Get your hands off me, Jasper! I won't be silenced!

*Bear One (Madame Poulet) takes her head off and approaches
the audience. She has a tiny body strapped to her chin.*

POULET

Ladies and gentlemen – I know it doesn't look like it, but
this is actually meant to happen –

LUDD

Don't tell them that! Ladies and gentlemen –

Bear Two tackles him again, bringing him to the floor.

Acting on the round stage

Acting in the round is a great leveller for actors. Any two actors sharing a round stage – however unequal the size of their roles – share equally the responsibility to communicate the play to an audience that entirely surrounds them. If a lead actor has their back to a section of audience for a longish period, observers can still learn lots by watching the reactive behaviour of the non-speaking messenger facing them. This actor with few or no lines to speak can add valuable information to a scene – including, perhaps, important subtext – simply by staying focused, listening, thinking, and reacting truthfully.

Audiences enjoy roughly equal status too. From a director's perspective, there's no point trying to get the picture right for one section of the audience since it will inevitably look wrong for people sitting opposite. A smart director sets a few basic guidelines then encourages the actors to behave pretty well as people do in real life.

That's not to suggest, however, that acting in the round requires no technique at all. Ben Kingsley again:

> You must have the energy in your body language and your vocal range to include the people sitting behind you. And how you do that is you bounce the energy off your fellow actor – he or she will then project your energy to the people sitting behind you. And you also can change your positions in a very graceful and elegant way.

If you've never acted in the round before, what's it like and – such as rules do exist – what are the rules? Stephen Joseph, when discussing round theatre acting, wrote of 'Action and reaction, the free use of the whole acting area for the actors to create three-dimensional images'. Joseph's simple statement captures the key element of round theatre performance: while the proscenium actor needs to be a highly skilled technician, the round theatre actor can concentrate more keenly on acting with, and reacting to, fellow performers.

Alan Ayckbourn has noted that actors new to the round stage tend to huddle together in the middle 'like nervous sheep in a thunderstorm'. The problem, of course, is that huddling actors facing inwards instinctively make their audience feel excluded. So you should generally try to keep actors apart 'unless they are kissing or punching each other' (Ayckbourn again). In fact, one of the curious magical qualities of working on a round stage is that two actors can be kept far apart – even on opposite sides of the stage – yet the watching audience will mentally shrink the distance so that a scene of great intimacy can still be played out. I'm not certain why it works, but it does. This is especially valuable because (generally speaking) the greater distance between actors, the more included the entire audience feels.

Always remember, of course, that in a naturalistic drama it should above all be the sincere thoughts, attitudes and feelings existing between characters that dictate the use space between actors. An actor who is relaxed and fully in character should be able to moderate their distance from other actors on a moment-by-moment basis. Even here though experience has shown that you need guidelines. Alan Ayckbourn has developed further tips on actors' movement on a theatre-in-the-round stage – including, 'Never return to the same place you started from' (because such a movement will feel like 'a loop' to the audience), and 'Don't keep standing up and sitting down' – because, as Ayckbourn puts it, 'psychologically that gives the audience the feeling that they're treading water'.

The sense of there being three dimensions is greater in round theatre than it is in a proscenium theatre. In fact, the three-dimensional aspect of round theatre comes into its own when the stage is rectangular. Suddenly there are corners for characters to hide in, to shrink from, to yearn to move into. The Arena Stage in Washington DC, with an entrance (or 'vom') at each of the four corners, stands as a good example of this. The square stage at the Stephen Joseph Theatre in Scarborough, England, features three irregularly placed voms. This, too, creates new and interesting space and shapes for actors to explore during rehearsals especially if lighting is to be used to create shadowy spaces onstage. Not that you need technology when you're exploring relationships between characters. There's value in periodically altering the way characters use space – including, crucially, by altering the extent to which characters turn physically towards each other. As in real life, a character who is unconfident or mistrusts another character may well turn away from them at a slight angle. A super-confident character will either present themselves full-on or may even turn fully away from the other character. (So too will a character who wants to seem superconfident.) In fact, the THOSE characteristics explored earlier (Tension, Height, Openness, Space and Eye-contact) can each be deployed to good and realistic effect, and with surprising subtlety, when you put two or more characters together on an intimate round or square stage.

Acting in space in training

If there are so many differences between acting for a proscenium stage and acting for a round stage – how then are actors prepared for this during their training?

It varies, of course, according to the training you receive. My own experience as a young actor in training was that almost all acting technique classes were run on the understanding that there was a fourth wall present – in other words, during any exercise that placed a single student actor in front of peers, the actor was asked to be aware that observers were sat on one side only. If you read the suggested classes and exercises outlined by established and highly regarded teachers from Stanislavski to Uta Hagen, they tend to assume that even private work takes place in this proscenium or endstage format. My own enquiries suggest that this situation continues within contemporary actor training.

I find this odd. If round theatre provides the actor with the most organic and least manipulated style of performing, shouldn't it be incorporated into performance training? An experienced acting teacher recently suggested to me that exposure to observers on all four sides would be too difficult for a training actor to cope with – but that a single audience/observer location (placed just beyond the invisible Fourth Wall) would be fully acceptable. My view, and my experience, is that any intensive acting exercise that requires observers to be present is always going to be less immersive for the student actor if they know they are only being watched from one side. If you pepper your disciplined observers all around the solo actor – in effect, beyond walls One, Two, Three and Four – this will reassure them that everything they do will reach someone. Nothing needs to be saved up and pushed out in a mono-directional line. Since teachers of naturalistic acting always require their students to participate in some sort of Stanislavskian 'solitude in public' exercise where the actor tries to create a sense of being alone while being watched, it surely makes sense to do so in an environment where the actor can behave as authentically as possible. Indeed, far from distracting the actors, the 'surrounding observers' approach can create a meditative atmosphere which intensifies the group's focus. In such an environment, I've seen visiting teachers slip away entirely unnoticed by the class.

Repertoire in the round

What though about choice of plays and styles of performance? An early criticism of round theatre in England, after its launch in 1955, was that you could only stage certain types of play in a round theatre space. Not so. Chekovian drama, tragi-comedy and family fantasy have been staged successfully for decades by Alan Ayckbourn; while Ben Kingsley – who 'can remember the whole of our audience in the round being completely enthralled by what we were doing' – remembers that under director Peter Cheeseman 'we did Ibsen, we did Shakespeare, we did classical theatre – we did some pretty strong stuff'. But what about, for example, Brecht-inspired work that relies on back-wall projection of words and images? Trickier in the round, I agree – though it's worth remembering that in a well-designed round theatre where the seating is quite steeply raked, the central stage floor can become, in effect, a backdrop. Depending on budgets it may also be possible to mount projector screens above the audience – perhaps even large-screen television monitors. Here's a thought though: if your live theatre event simply cannot take place without a back-wall screen for projection, then perhaps it's actually cinema you're trying to create?

It's perhaps worth noting too that theatre-in-the-round can be staged very cheaply indeed. In fact, if you can manage without lighting, you don't even need a theatre! A typical community hall can easily and temporarily be converted within a very short time. A square stage (perhaps twenty feet square) with irregular exit points will provide you with an interesting space to work with. A front row of chairs, and a second row of strong tables, can provide you with raked seating for perhaps seventy people. You can get away with virtually no set and minimal props – in fact you'll need to since large items will hamper audience sightlines. As in the Commedia dell'arte and Globe Theatre days of old, you might want instead to save your money for impressive costumes that look good close-up. You might also choose to invest your spare cash in extra rehearsal time – making sure your actors know their characters, can find the right acting style at the right moment, and can make sophisticated use of the square stage.

In fact, you don't even need a formal script to make round theatre work for you. You may already have encountered Augusto Boal's **Forum Theatre**. This socially valuable theatre tool allows audience members to intervene directly in a short conflict-based play – changing, as it were, the course of events in a tragedy while simultaneously gaining valuable practice at being assertive.

If you've ever experienced Forum Theatre you'll know that ordinary audience members often don't to want to intervene and become spectactors (as Boal called them) if they feel they also need to be skilled performers. Audiences can also be put off by the prospect of a longish journey from seat to stage. A round theatre staging almost entirely removes this fear, especially for those sat on or near the front row. And once onstage, spectactors encounter an untheatrical realism that can quickly immerse everyone in the conflict. It's all the more surprising, perhaps, that forum-style theatre is rarely performed fully in the round. Incidentally, fun improvisation work can work really well in the round too. As in scripted work, the onstage experience discourages showboating and encourages ensemble work. So, if you're a practitioner who has used these methods, but never in the round, why not give it a go?

final thoughts

All actors, especially transformational character actors, need a reliable technique. It's important to have something to fall back on if the direction you are receiving in the rehearsal room is unhelpful or if your character starts to (unintentionally) become a caricature or if spontaneity in performance starts to wane. But not everyone will want to approach acting in the type of structured way offered in this book. You will be expected to employ detective skills and show an ongoing willingness to analyse, reflect and experiment. The 'Planning to Act' stage in particular can be hard work though it really does pay dividends. Anyway, there it is – some tools, some practical techniques, some thoughts on how to be more versatile and more effective as an actor. Some of it, perhaps most of it, you will have encountered in some form elsewhere. Whether that's the case or not, I hope I have at least helped to clear the water in a pool that can get very clouded indeed.

Those of us who train student actors have a responsibility to empower them, to enable them to eventually function just as well, or better, without their teachers. Acting is a public activity so actors in training need an audience to complete the essential triangle of 'A's which all theatre needs – **Author**, **Actor** and **Audience** – and public speaking, which is a massive part of acting in public, makes people nervous. So whether you're using this book as a self-help guide or working with a teacher, you really do need to practise doing what you do in front of a live audience. An actor who is unaccustomed to an audience can seem to resent their presence. That's disrespectful and an audience feels it. If they like your performance you'll know because, with practice, you'll sense it (well before the curtain call). But if an audience can't follow your communication – especially if they can't hear your words – one way or another they'll tell you. That's another reason for the planning described in this book. If you're concentrating hard on your objective and you're emotionally in role, then you're not worrying about what the person on the front row thinks of your acting.

In summary then here's how to deliver an excellent transformational character acting performance. Plan like an actor possessed. Experiment in rehearsal and in private with the vigour and playfulness of a young child. Then, on the day of performance, be properly warmed up, be appropriately in character and in scene, and have a clear sense of the degree of vocal projection and diction required to reach the most distant audience member. Have confidence in all you've been doing to prepare, then go out and forget the detail – *all of it* – trusting instead to your skill as a spontaneous human being. And if you want to be really versatile as a transformational character actor then remember – consciously at first then unconsciously in performance – to:

use	
t	(tension)
h	(height)
o	(openness)
s	(space)
e	(eye contact)
l	(loudness)
i	(inflection)
n	(note)
t	(tone)
p	(pace)
a	(accent)
d	(diction)
s	(specials)

appendix

Guidelines on filling in a Character Profile Sheet

Fill in a copy of the Character Profile Sheet on the next page each time you start work on a new character. Use a pencil so that you can make changes (you may also need a highlighter pen).

Begin by sifting the script – you're looking for clues to your character. Then keep the sheet with you as rehearsals progress, adding and altering as you make new discoveries.

The sheet is in sections and, once you've listed the key facts down the left hand side, the rest of the sheet can be completed in pretty well any order. Mostly it's self-explanatory, but below are some further guidelines which might help:

- *Favourite Fantasy:* this invites you to identify or (when you know the character well enough) invent a secret fantasy for your character. As well as helping you to add depth in understanding your character, this section also provides (time permitting) the basis for a provocative improvisation: what would the experience be like if your character's fantasy came true? If you were playing a servant who fantasises about being king, the experience of being served and lauded by everyone else in the story would be a powerful imagined memory.

- *Lifetime Objective:* this is an overarching 'want' that drives your character's overall behaviour at this point in their life. This is likely to be something which remains the same, unless some massive incident impacts on your character's life to change the lifetime objective. Examples are, 'to be famous', 'to help others', 'to do everything once before I die'. Unlike the Favourite Fantasy section, your character must believe that this Lifetime Objective is achievable.

- *Status seesaw:* this section allows you to visualise your character's relationship with a second significant character in the script at the point when the characters are first seen together. There is a thin plank already drawn in on the seesaw. Draw a new one which shows the balance of status between your character and the other person. The angle of the plank indicates, at a glance, the degree of relative status.

- *Nickname:* this can be a useful aide-memoire when acting a character, as a nickname is usually a potted descriptive label for a character's personality, whether it be 'Brains', 'Trouble', 'Sunshine' or whatever. Obviously nicknames which are simply words derived from a person's name rarely have any value in giving you a feel for the character. In truth you'll probably often need to make up the nickname. If so, leave the nicknaming until last so that you have all the information you need to create a suitable one. And remember – we don't choose our own nicknames.

- *Personality test:* use a highlighter pen, or circle with your pencil, to record the qualities, traits and attitudes you confidently feel are shown by your character at some point in the play. The behaviour only has to be observed once. You'll almost certainly find interesting paradoxes and conflicts: a character may seem carefree one moment, pessimistic the next; peaceful here, but restless two pages on (or even in the same scene). This section will help you to avoid stereotyping – like real people, well-written characters are complex creatures whose moods and thoughts can change radically and without notice. And their behaviour may well alter in direct response to the company they keep. When you've filled in all the behaviours which your character shows in the play, you'll notice that there are more words

NAME .... **Nickname** ....

Favourite Fantasy ....

FACTS
(include age, family, social position)

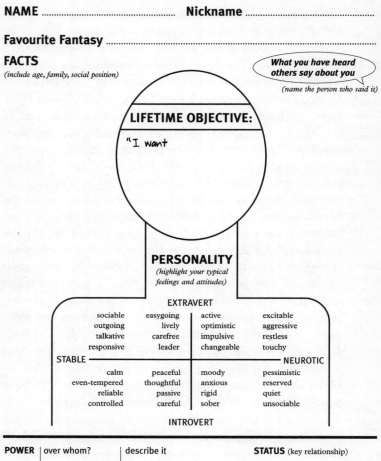

What you have heard
others say about you

(name the person who said it)

LIFETIME OBJECTIVE:

"I want

PERSONALITY
*(highlight your typical
feelings and attitudes)*

EXTRAVERT

sociable	easygoing	active	excitable
outgoing	lively	optimistic	aggressive
talkative	carefree	impulsive	restless
responsive	leader	changeable	touchy

STABLE ———————————————————— NEUROTIC

calm	peaceful	moody	pessimistic
even-tempered	thoughtful	anxious	reserved
reliable	passive	rigid	quiet
controlled	careful	sober	unsociable

INTROVERT

POWER	over whom?	describe it
Agreed		
Abuse		
Reward		
Information		
Connection		
Personal		

STATUS (key relationship)

Name of individual ....

STATUS SEESAW

My status   Their status

(draw in balance of status)

NAME ..Natasha.......................... **Nickname** Miss Bossyboots

from 'Three Sisters' by Chekhov

Favourite Fantasy ...Being guest of honour at a grand ball........

FACTS

(include age, family, social position)

- local girl
- engaged to, then marries Andrei
- gains wealth through marriage
- runs the house once married
- becomes mother to Sophie and Bobik
- husband is would-be academic & gambler
- considered by some to have married above class
- learns French (Andrei's sisters speak other languages too)
- believes that servants should be sacked when too old to work at previous standard
- begins an affair with Protopopov

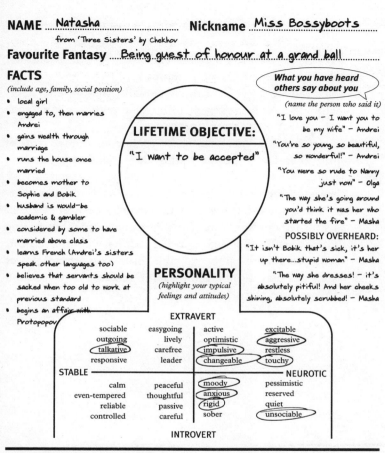

LIFETIME OBJECTIVE:

"I want to be accepted"

PERSONALITY
(highlight your typical feelings and attitudes)

EXTRAVERT

sociable	easygoing	active	excitable
outgoing	lively	optimistic	aggressive
talkative	carefree	impulsive	restless
responsive	leader	changeable	touchy

STABLE ———————————————— NEUROTIC

calm	peaceful	moody	pessimistic
even-tempered	thoughtful	anxious	reserved
reliable	passive	rigid	quiet
controlled	careful	sober	unsociable

INTROVERT

What you have heard others say about you

(name the person who said it)

"I love you — I want you to be my wife" — Andrei

"You're so young, so beautiful, so wonderful!" — Andrei

"You were so rude to Nanny just now" — Olga

"The way she's going around you'd think it was her who started the fire" — Masha

POSSIBLY OVERHEARD:

"It isn't Bobik that's sick, it's her up there...stupid woman" — Masha

"The way she dresses! — it's absolutely pitiful! And her cheeks shining, absolutely scrubbed!" — Masha

POWER	over whom?	describe it
Agreed	the servants	orders them about
Abuse	the sisters & servants	loses her temper and threatens their rights*
Reward	Andrei and the children	gives them love and attention (and withdraws it)
Information	the sisters	she gains experience in raising children
Connection	the sisters/Andrei	gains higher social status through marriage
Personal	Andrei and Protopopov	considered very attractive

* has the power to sack Anfisa; demands that Irina give up her bedroom

STATUS (key relationship)

Name of individual ...Masha..................

STATUS SEESAW

My status   Their status

(draw in balance of status)

(feels socially inferior and feels Masha looks down on her)

highlighted (or circled) in one quarter of the diagram than in others. You can conclude from this whether your character is, on balance, a stable extrovert, say, or a neurotic introvert (or a different combination). This gives you a quick-reference sense of the personality of your character, including to what extent their personality differs from your own.

- *Power:* this is a quick-reference section to remind you of your character's power within key relationships. This section, brief though it is, can be crucial in affecting your character's behaviour towards others since both your character and the other person will normally be well aware of each other's power, and of the consequences of exercising that power. If other actors in the cast have completed this section too, there can be valuable discussion around power issues in a play. If time allows, some valuable improvisation can also take place.

Relaxation Exercise with Visualisation

Wear loose, comfortable clothes. Remove your shoes and lie flat on your back on a soft floor in a warm, quiet room. If you want to you can tuck a soft pillow or similar under your neck, and you can raise your knees, too, if you find it more comfortable.

Shut your eyes and allow yourself to breathe at a normal pace and depth. Let your stomach rise and fall as you breathe.

Imagine you're lying on a giant, strong, supportive, but soft sponge. The muscle tension in your body is something you want to be rid of. Visualise it as a coloured liquid or gel which will sink into the sponge below you if you let it.

Start by tensing your toes. Imagine your feet are claws, toes curled downwards. Hold this position for a count of ten, then relax. As you relax, visualise the tension which you were holding in your toes draining away into the sponge below you.

Now curl your toes upwards. Visualise the tension held in your muscles. After counting silently to ten, relax, letting the tension drain away into the sponge below you.

Work systematically through your body in this way, tensing and relaxing the muscles in this order: ankles; legs below the knee; knees; thighs; bottom; lower back; stomach; upper back; chest; shoulders; hands (make them into tight fists then spread your fingers wide as if you have webbed hands); wrists; forearms; elbows; upper arms; shoulders again; neck (tense only gently); face (make your face as small as you possibly can then spread your features as wide as you can).

When everything has been tense and relaxed, make a mental check of whether any tension has crept back in. If you think it may have, mentally isolate that part of your body and repeat the exercise locally using the visualisation.

As you lie there, try to remember just how this state of being fully relaxed feels.

In your own time, slowly raise yourself from this relaxed state so that you are standing. Be conscious of using only the muscles which are necessary for standing.

Accents Scrapbook: an example

Here's an example of a possible scrapbook entry for the UK **Liverpool accent**:

Loudness – no specific trait, can be loud or soft or in between. The caricature Scouser speaks loudly, but in reality there are plenty of quiet Scouse voices.

Inflection – Scouse has a definite and recognisable inflection pattern, which tends to have repeating patterns. The inflection pattern is often confused with that of the Birmingham accent, but there are subtle differences. Scousers tend to use a narrower-than-normal range of notes in normal speech.

Note – no specific trait other than that male speakers can tend towards use of a higher note as part of the exciteable quality of this urban accent.

Tone – tends to be hard, caused by some tension towards the back of the throat and on the soft palate (on the roof of the mouth nearer the throat).

Pace – tends to be fast, part of the speaker's identity for being quick-witted. Individual words can habitually glide into the 'er' sound to allow the speaker thinking time such as 'so – er'; but this quickly slides into stereotyping unless the actor is vigilant.

Diction – tends to be fairly poor, caused in part by habitual limited use of the mouth and lips to form words. There's a 'splashiness' to certain sounds – the word 'hat' can come out as almost 'hats' with a soft 't'. 'Great' can sound almost like 'grace'. The hard 'c' and 'k' sounds can sound splashy at the end of a word, so that 'kick' can sound like 'kikh', with the hard sound at the end of the word being held momentarily on the soft palate.

Specials – thick 's' sounds are common, often as a result of only limited use of the tongue during speech. The tongue may protrude minutely through the teeth.

Words – certain words are substituted when compared with standard English. 'We did it' may come out as 'we done it'; 'we didn't' can become 'we never'.

Famous speakers: the Beatles; recent example – footballer Steven Gerrard.

Further reading

An Actor Prepares – Konstantin Stanislavski (Methuen Drama)

Building a Character – Konstantin Stanislavski (Methuen Drama)

Clear Speech – Malcolm Morrison (Methuen Drama)

Confusions: Acting Edition S. – Alan Ayckbourn (Samuel French Ltd)

English Phonetics and Phonology: A Practical Course – Peter Roach (Cambridge University Press)

Impro: Improvisation and the Theatre – Keith Johnstone (Methuen Drama)

In the Company of Actors – Carole Zucker (Methuen Drama)

John Godber Plays: Bouncers, Happy Families, Shakers – John Godber (Methuen Drama)

Mindwatching – Hans and Michael Eysenck (Book Club Associates)

The Pocket Guide to Manwatching – Desmond Morris (Triad Books)

True and False: Heresy and Common Sense for the Actor – David Mamet (Faber and Faber)

Voice and the Actor – Cicely Berry (Virgin Books)

Official website for H J Eysenck:
http://freespace.virgin.net/darrin.evans

Amiina.com:
I discovered this Icelandic group a couple of years back. They produce quirkily beautiful music that has the uncanny ability to put you in a calm mood – and if necessary send you to sleep!

Official website for the author: www.paulelsam.com

glossary

Abuse power is power which a person uses to force another person to do something (e.g. a school bully threatens to hurt another child unless money is handed over). Abuse power is also used when a person with Agreed power abuses their authority (e.g. a doctor inappropriately asks a patient to strip naked).

Accent is a characteristic of voice and speech which reveals where you are likely to have been brought up, and/or which social class you belong to. Each regional accent can be deconstructed to assess its typical characteristics using the criteria of Loudness, Inflection, Note, Tone, Pace, Diction and 'Specials'.

Agreed power is power which a person is allowed to use as a result of their position within a culture (e.g. a manager can ask a junior member of a team to carry out a duty; a police officer is allowed to arrest a suspect; a parent might stop a child's pocket money as a punishment).

Ayckbourn, Sir Alan was for many years Artistic Director of the Stephen Joseph Theatre in Scarborough. A Tony, Olivier and Moliere-award-winning playwright, he is one of the world's most widely performed writers, creating work for adult audiences (including *Confusions*, *Season's Greetings*, *The Norman Conquests* and *Joking Apart*), and for family audiences (including *My Very Own Story* and *The Champion of Paribanou*).

Beckett, Samuel was an Irish-born Nobel Prize-winning absurdist playwright whose theatre experiments ranged from *Waiting* *for Godot*, in which two tramps wait for someone called Godot who never arrives, to *Not I*, in which the only thing seen is the carefully lit mouth of the solo actor. Often writing in French, Beckett's other plays include *Endgame*, *Krapp's Last Tape* and *Happy Days*.

Berkoff, Steven is a controversial London-born playwright, director and actor whose highly stylised plays include *East, West, Decadence, Sink the Belgrano* and *Messiah*. Adaptations include Kafka's *The Trial* and Edgar Allan Poe's *The Fall of the House of Usher*. Berkoff has also worked widely on screen, often playing a villain.

Character actor is a term most often used to describe an older actor who makes their living portraying one key character type, e.g. 'The Tough Guy', 'The Grumpy Old Woman'. In films their character is often a supporting character to the lead actor(s), so there are few really famous character actors.

Chekhov, Anton was a provocative Russian playwright working at the forefront of social realist theatre in the late nineteenth century. Plays include *The Seagull, The Cherry Orchard, The Three Sisters*, and *Uncle Vanya*. Chekhov is also revered for his short stories.

Chekhov, Michael was a Russian-born teacher, actor, director and theorist and former student of Stanislavski. A nephew to Anton Chekhov, he left Russia for England, where he founded an Acting Studio which later relocated to the United States. His experimental work with actors led to the development of new approaches to acting, which were partially eclipsed in the USA by 'The Method'.

Classicist actors are drawn to text which is filled with imagery and is challenging to deliver. They enjoy a sense of comfort with the textual style of 'the classics'. At best, they combine the skills of the Inhabiter and the Storyteller to tell a character's story truthfully. At worst, they can overindulge in the poetry of the text. Their skill combines the best of the other two types, but adds a sense of fearlessness towards difficult text.

Connection power is power which comes from being close to someone who has power (e.g. a school pupil is the daughter of the headmaster; you have a friend who is a famous film actor).

Diction means clarity of speech. Clear speech, which is essential for actors, is achieved mainly through a combination of active use of the muscles involved in speech – mainly the lips – and through a relaxed yet energised ability to project your voice effectively, including projection of the sounds made when vowels are used in speech.

Diphthong occurs when one vowel sound slides into another with no consonant in between. The word 'boy' is an example of a particularly strong diphthong, which, in English Received Pronunciation, slides from the sound which you get in the middle of the word 'good' to the sound that you get in the middle of the word 'hit'. Short words such as 'go' are diphthongs, as are 'may' and 'hear'. Diphthong sounds often vary greatly from accent to accent.

Emotion memory describes a rehearsal and performance activity in which an actor tackles a moment in the story of their character by imaginatively provoking memories of one or more analogous situations from the actor's own life. Ideally the revisiting of a personal emotional experience will be read by the audience as a true emotional response of the character to the story.

Eye contact describes how we use our eyes to observe things and to interpret other people. We also use it to signal or disguise our own feelings and intentions. The direction and the duration of eye contact between people is significant. Continuous eye contact (staring), no eye contact, and flickered eye contact (when people look up briefly then quickly look away) are all significant in revealing a person's confidence and their sense of relative status.

Eysenck, Hans – the late psychologist, researcher and writer whose substantial body of work includes *Mindwatching* and *Know Your Own Personality*. (See Further Reading for a link to the Eysenck website.)

Glottal stop is a characteristic of voice and speech in which voiced outward breath is momentarily trapped in the throat. Common to accents such as London Cockney and Newcastle Geordie, the glottal stop acts as a substitute for a consonant in a word or phrase – usually the 't' sound – so that 'bottle' becomes 'bo'l'.

Godber, John is a playwright and former Artistic Director of Hull Truck Theatre in Hull, East Yorkshire. Plays include *Bouncers*, *Up 'n' Under*, *Teechers* and *Shakers* (co-written with Jane Thornton). Musicals include *Thick as a Brick* and the family musical *Big Trouble in the Little Bedroom*.

Gogol, Nickolai was a Russian writer whose works include the darkly witty 1836 play *The Government Inspector* (frequently revived in adapted form – e.g. at the National Theatre in London as *The UN Inspector*) and the novel *Dead Souls*.

Height describes, for the purposes of this book, a person's manipulated height, as compared to their natural height. The reasons why they manipulate their height so that it differs from their natural height may be straightforward (e.g. they sit because they are tired) or psychologically significant (e.g. they sit because they are acknowledging their lower status compared to another person who stands).

Humanimal is another word for the human being. The author uses the term as a way of reminding the reader that, beneath our sophisticated veneer, we are still animals with all the basic urges and needs that go with that condition. For instance, while most humans no longer hunt for their own food, they do still fight for status and power in society.

Inflection describes the way in which we move through different note patterns when use our voices. We alter inflection to add meaning: it helps the listener to understand what we are saying and to prioritise the importance of the different words we speak. Inflection is also used to express feeling, for example through a yawn or through laughter. The degree of inflection a person uses can reveal significant things about their state of mind.

Inhabiter actors need to become a character. They work hard to engage psychologically and emotionally with the circumstances within a character's story. At best they can be deeply moving for an audience to observe; at worst, they can be resentful of an audience's presence, which may damage their effectiveness as communicators.

Inner life refers to the psychological and emotional activity which an actor is involved in during rehearsal and performance. Sometimes this inner activity will be clearly expressed through spontaneous non-verbal behaviour; at other times an audience will unconsciously sense, perhaps through some emotional quality in an actor's voice, that the actor is experiencing intense thought and feeling.

Johnstone, Keith is a teacher, writer and director who has pioneered techniques for improvisation, initially through his work at the Royal Court Theatre in London. A Professor Emeritus at the University of Calgary, he is co-founder of the Loose Moose theatre company and has written the books *Impro* and *Impro for Storytellers*.

Joseph, Stephen was a radical English director and theatre manager who promoted the experience of theatre-going to non-traditional audiences. Joseph brought theatre-in-the-round to the UK, and supported a range of young theatremakers including Alan Ayckbourn, Peter Cheeseman and Harold Pinter.

Knowledge power is power which comes from having information or expertise which is needed by someone else (e.g. a homeless person knows the location of the nearest taxi rank; a technician is able to repair a computer problem).

Labelling is the process by which a person's sense of identity alters as a result of the way they are treated by others, so a person who is regarded by others as having no common sense may well start to share that belief. Their altered belief then translates into altered behaviour so that they may for example become less confident and more indecisive.

Loudness refers to vocal loudness or volume, which can reveal important psychological things about a person. Confident people are often loud; shy people are often quiet. Vocal volume becomes interesting when people's preferred volume is inappropriate – when a shy person is public speaking for example. People may also manipulate their volume for effect: the super-confident person trying to attract a shy person may adopt a quieter more intimate vocal level.

Lifetime objective is an overarching want that drives a character's overall behaviour. This is likely to be something that remains the same unless some massive incident impacts on the character's life to change the lifetime objective. Examples are 'to be famous', 'to help others', 'to do everything once before I die'.

Magic What If? refers to Stanislavski's idea that convincing, truthful acting needs to be provoked imaginatively. Any situation faced by a character in a play can be explored using an empathetic imaginative approach in which actors place themselves in that imagined situation and respond spontaneously to it.

Mamet, David is an American playwright, director and screenwriter whose plays include *Oleanna, The Duck Variations, Sexual Perversity in Chicago, American Buffalo* and *Glengarry Glen Ross*, for which he was awarded the Pulitzer Prize in 1984. Books include *True and False*.

Method acting is a phrase most often used to refer to the style of acting which demands that an actor should always experience, and re-experience, true, spontaneous emotion during performance. Adapted from the teachings of Stanislavski, 'The Method' is credited most of all to the American actor, teacher and director Lee Strasberg.

Miller, Arthur was a Pulitzer Prize-winning American playwright whose plays include *The Crucible, All My Sons, A View from the Bridge* and *Death of a Salesman*. His plays continued to be performed even after his blacklisting by the House Un-American Activities Committee. After the Hollywood Blacklist was lifted, Miller wrote the screenplay for the film *The Misfits*.

Note describes the individual sound which combines with other sounds to form inflection. Unlike in singing or in music, a vocal note is never in- or out-of-tune since the voice spontaneously uses an infinitely wide range of notes including the areas between notes on the traditional musical scale.

Objective is a term describing what a character is fighting to achieve at any given moment in a scene. When a script has been divided into units, the actor views each unit from their character's perspective and tries to work out what the character is trying to achieve in relation to others. Each discrete 'want' becomes the character's specific objective in each unit. Examples of playable objectives include, 'I want to make you smile' and 'I want you to leave the room'.

Olivier, Laurence was a British-born Oscar-winning transformational character actor and co-founder of the National Theatre in London who performed widely on the stage as well as on screen. Films include *Rebecca*, *Wuthering Heights*, *The Marathon Man* and Shakespeare's *Henry V*. He became Lord Olivier in 1971.

Openness describes the degree to which we open up or conceal the front of the body. Standing 'fully open' means legs apart, head raised, arms away from torso (e.g. hands on hips) while 'fully closed' means legs entwined, head tilted down, arms folded tightly across chest or stomach. The degree of openness is one of the most influential bodily signs – you can make a strong initial judgement on a person's state of mind by looking at their openness from some distance away. The ultimate degree of concealment and self-protection is the foetal position.

Pace describes the speed at which speech takes place. As with most personal characteristics, speed of speech creates different perceptions of the speaker. Fast speech can suggest confidence, quick-wittedness, spontaneity, energy. Slow speech can suggest reticence, low intelligence, cautiousness, listlessness. But fast speech can also suggest nervousness and slow speech can be the sign of a confident person who chooses to dictate the pace of communication.

Personal power is power which comes from a person's attractiveness to others either because of their looks or their personality (e.g. a model, or a member of a group who can tell jokes brilliantly).

Phonetic alphabet is the alphabet of sounds which experts use to deconstruct speech. The phonetic alphabet can be invaluable in helping actors to master accents, but the actor must be willing to learn a wide range of symbols from this alphabet and will need a good ear to hear the subtle differences between sounds in any given accent.

Physical barrier is a practical obstruction that hampers a character's ability to achieve an objective. If the objective is 'I want to know if you are lying', physical barriers might be 'but I can't see your eyes behind your sunglasses' or 'I can't hear your tone of voice well enough over the noise from traffic'.

Physical status is a term used to describe how a person's non-verbal behaviour automatically claims a position for them on the status seesaw. Tension, height, openness, use of space, and eye contact (THOSE) can all be altered to claim a lower or higher position in relation to another person.

Pinter, Harold was a Nobel Prize-winning playwright, director and actor whose plays include *The Birthday Party*, *The Caretaker*, *Betrayal*, *One for the Road* and *The Hothouse*. Screenplays include *The Go-Between* and *The French Lieutenant's Woman*.

Psychological barrier is a thought or feeling that hampers a character's ability to achieve the objective they are fighting for. If the objective is 'I want to kiss you', psychological barriers might be, say, 'but I'm not sure you find me attractive' or 'but I'm married'.

Received Pronunciation (or RP) is a supposedly neutral accent used by some speakers in the UK that comprises sounds that are not specific to any particular region. Once common to UK-based broadcasters and actors (who were trained to use RP as their everyday accent), the accent nowadays tends simply to identify (untrained) speakers as being from a non-working class background.

Relaxation means shedding the body of as much unnecessary muscular tension as possible. Actors often put themselves through a structured relaxation prior to performance (see 'Relaxation Exercise with Visualisation' in the Appendix) to help them feel focused and in control and to help them build the physical and psychological profile of their character.

Representational acting is now mostly used as a term of disparagement to describe an outdated style of acting in which stylised movement and poetical vocal delivery was preferred over spontaneous, emotional truthfulness. The performances in the early-to-mid twentieth century by English actors such as the young John Gielgud and Noel Coward stand as examples. The term has also been used to describe actors whose skilful performances do not require the actor to experience constant emotion.

Resonators are chambers of varying size which are situated throughout the upper body. They include the mouth, nose, throat and lungs, and also the sinuses – tiny chambers peppered around the skull. Each of these resonators has the potential to help the voice to be amplified and to enhance tone.

Reward power describes the power to supply something which is valued by another person (e.g. an interviewer rewards a candidate with a job; a parent rewards a child with a sweet; a child rewards a parent with a smile).

Russell, Willy is a Liverpool-born playwright whose stage plays include *Our Day Out, Stags and Hens, Shirley Valentine* and *Educating Rita* (the last two were also made into films). He also wrote the book, words and music for the musical *Blood Brothers*.

Seesaw principle refers to Keith Johnstone's stated rule-of-thumb which dictates that the raising of a person's status will always simultaneously lower the status of someone or something else, and vice versa.

Sellers, Peter was an acclaimed British transformational character actor whose films include *Being There, I'm Alright Jack* and the Pink Panther series. In the Stanley Kubrick film *Doctor Strangelove* he convincingly portrayed three wildly differing central characters.

Sense memory describes a rehearsal and performance activity in which an actor achieves a sense of truthfulness during a moment in the story of their character by provoking themselves with memories of analogous situations from their own life in which some combination of the five senses was intensely experienced. Ideally the revisiting of a sensory memory from the actor's own life will add authenticity to the actor's performance.

Shakespeare, William was an English-born Elizabethan playwright and actor whose works between 1588 and 1616 include *Hamlet*, *King Lear*, *The Tempest*, *Comedy of Errors* and *A Midsummer Night's Dream*. He is also known for his prolific output of Sonnets.

Showreel is a DVD or website address showcasing the previous work of an actor for the benefit of casting directors, agents and directors. This will normally be edited to feature only scenes from productions in which the actor appears, and ideally will contain only professional work in which the actor can be viewed performing dialogue.

Social status attaches to a person as a result of how society views people in their position. In this hierarchy a king is deemed more important than a bank manager, but the bank manager has higher social status than an office cleaner who has higher social status than someone who is long-term unemployed. Your normal social status is always lurking there in the background when people interact with you and it has much to do with power. The more power you have to influence others, the higher up the social hierarchy you will be.

Space is the area surrounding your body which you use or decide not to use. In this book we are concerned with how you move within space when other people are nearby – how much, or how little, physical space you claim. It can be visualised as a flexible invisible bubble which each person carries with them.

People claim space through their bodily size and movement, and through their attitude, so to understand space in relation to bodies you need to be familiar with the other four characteristics of movement – tension, height, openness and eye contact. All four variables allow you to claim or abandon the space which another person might want.

Specials are common idiosyncrasies of speech. They include substitution of the sounds 'f' for 'th' ('fink' instead of 'think'); difficulty pronouncing the strong 'r' (so that 'worry' becomes 'wowy'); mispronunciation of the 's' sound to produce something like a 'th' ('thith-ter' instead of 'sister'); and the glottal stop.

Spontaneity is an important goal for all actors. It represents the achievement of the act of imaginatively living in the moment during a performance. Achieving spontaneity brings with it an ease which enables the actor, and fellow actors, to make correct and truthful choices during performance. If all actors in a scene are achieving spontaneity in a scene the performance will seem to light up emotionally. However, the actors must remember to maintain good technique (e.g. voice projection) even while achieving imaginative spontaneity.

Spotlight is the UK directory of actors' photographs which is published annually. The publication is aimed at (and issued to) directors and casting directors, to help them with the casting process. *Spotlight* is published online as well as in print. (See also *The Actors' Yearbook* published by Methuen Drama).

Stanislavski, Konstantin was a Russian-born actor, director, writer and theorist who developed the first systematic approach to naturalistic acting in the early twentieth century. Books include *An Actor Prepares*, *Being a Character*, *My Life in Art*. His influence on acting in the West remains strong to this day.

Storyteller actors enjoy telling the story of the play to the audience. Communication is focused primarily on this task, and even if they never actually look at the audience they are always aware of them, reaching through the divide to share a character's experience. From the audience's perspective, at best Storyteller actors can be hugely entertaining performers; at worst, they can lack engagement with fellow actors and can lack truth.

Strasberg, Lee was an American teacher, actor, director and theorist whose work with former students of Stanislavski led to the formation of the New York-based Acting Studio, and the development of the American Method (sometimes aka 'The Method') approach to acting.

Subtext describes the thoughts and motivations which lie behind the words spoken by a character. Modern playwrights almost always disguise some of their characters' true thoughts and intentions in order to achieve a sense of psychological realism. Actors need to be sensitised to this.

Tension is a word to describe the presence of tensed muscles in the body. At any given moment muscles are tightened or relaxed. The amount of tension, and the degree to which muscles are tensed when it is not physically essential, reveals something significant about the psychological state of the individual.

Tone describes the degree of hardness or softness in the quality of a person's voice. It is altered as a result of three key factors in the body: how relaxed the muscles are around the voice-amplifying resonators; how freely the breath flows during speech; and where the note is pitched. These three factors are interrelated so that a soft tone will typically occur if a low note is used to breathe freely through a relaxed upper body.

Transactional analysis is a theory in which verbal status behaviour falls into one of three types: adult, parent or child. It is suggested that in speech we unconsciously select one of these roles to communicate, and that we often choose a role which is at odds with our social status. A parent might spontaneously adopt child behaviour by losing emotional control and throwing a tantrum. The same person, at work as a teacher, might nurture an adult-to-adult way of working with students.

Transformational character actor is an actor who is skilled in greatly altering physical and vocal characteristics to enable them to inhabit a range of characters. Examples include Peter Sellers, Daniel Day Lewis, Meryl Streep, Michael Sheen.

True root note is the natural vocal note which you make when you're fully relaxed, for example when you vocalise a yawn in private. People have different root notes, both for physiological reasons (determined mainly by size and tension within the vocal cords) and psychological reasons (when people become socialised into vocally adapting to ways other people expect them to behave).

Unit is a term used to describe a small section of script (perhaps half a page) in which each of the characters in a scene is engaged in a single significant objective or 'want'. When there is a change in circumstances – e.g. a character in the story enters or leaves, or one character starts to push for something new within the scene – that unit ends and the next one begins.

Verbal status is a term used to describe how a speaker's choice of words, and the attitude behind those words, automatically claim a position for the speaker on the status seesaw. If two people on the imaginary seesaw have opposite social status – a king and a tramp, for example – then verbal status activity can instantly undermine the established relative social status and so change the overall status balance. Higher status can be claimed either by lowering that of the other person (e.g. by insulting them) or by raising your own (e.g. by praising yourself).

Visualisation is the technique of harnessing the imagination to mentally see something happen. Visualisation is used to build self-confidence or to prepare for an experience. For an actor this might mean anything from using visualisation to improve relaxation skill (see Relaxation Exercise with Visualisation in the Appendix) to visualising an intense and significant in-character moment which occurs away from the script.

index